Biblical

THE QUESTIONS WE HAVE

Keys

AND THE ANSWERS WE NEED

To Life

LATINA NICHOLE SMITH

LUVHEIR
PUBLISHING

Unless otherwise indicated, all Scripture references and quotations are taken from *The Living Bible* (TLB), copyright © 1971 by Tyndale House Foundation. Used by permission of Tyndale House Publishers, Carol Stream, Illinois 60188. All rights reserved. Scriptures marked NKJV are taken from the New King James Version®. Copyright © 1982 by Thomas Nelson. Used by permission. All rights reserved. Scriptures marked NLT are taken from the *Holy Bible*, New Living Translation. Copyright© 1996, 2004, 2015 by Tyndale House Foundation. Used by permission of Tyndale House Publishers, Carol Stream, Illinois 60188. All rights reserved. Scriptures marked NIV are taken from the Holy Bible, New International Version®, NIV®. Copyright © 1973, 1978, 1984, 2011 by Biblica, Inc.™ Used by permission of Zondervan. All rights reserved worldwide. www.zondervan.com. Scriptures marked AMP are taken from the Amplified Bible. Copyright © 2015 by The Lockman Foundation. Used by permission.

Any *quote* of scripture that does not include a version in the reference incorporates verbiage from more than one version.

Disclaimer and Waiver of Liability

This book is intended to educate, inspire, and empower. Although the recommendations in this book have been proven successful, results vary by individual. The author and publisher shall have neither liability nor responsibility to anyone with respect to any loss or damage caused or alleged to be caused directly or indirectly by the information contained in this book.

Publisher's Cataloging-in-Publication data

Names: Smith, Latina Nichole, author.
Title: Biblical keys to life : the questions we have and the answers we need / Latina Nichole Smith.
Description: Includes index. | Astor, FL: Luvheir Publishing, 2022.
Identifiers: LCCN: 2022912994 | ISBN: 9781958966006 (hardcover) | 9781958966013 (paperback) | 9781958966020 (audio) | 9781958966037 (ebook)
Subjects: LCSH Happiness--Religious aspects--Christianity. | Well-being--Religious aspects--Christianity. | Christian life. | BISAC RELIGION / Christian Living / Personal Growth | RELIGION / Christian Living / Spiritual Growth
Classification: LCC BV4647.J68 .S65 2022 | DDC 248.4--dc23

Printed in the United States of America

For information on bulk order discounts, speaking events, or other inquiries, email:
info@LuvheirPublishing.com

This book is dedicated to
my Heavenly Father and my three children,
Sean, Alanna, and Laila, who are my heart's joy
and my inspiration for writing this book.

Also, for truth seekers all over the world
—this one's for you.

Contents

"I am the Light of the world.
So if you follow me, you won't be stumbling through
the darkness, for living light will flood your path."
- Jesus
John 8:12 TLB

Escaping Dysfunction and Finding Answers

T he world seems to be getting crazier and crazier by the day. Confusion, depression, anxiety, toxicity, nonsense, and madness are at an all time high. What's really going on in the world?

This is just one of the many questions we find ourselves asking on a regular basis. Along with: What's the point of life? What's the truth about God? What's wrong with people? How can we find true happiness? And the list goes on. The same questions have been circulating for centuries. But now—it's time for answers, and it's time for solutions.

By the end of this book, you will have a solid understanding of God, life, and people, including yourself. This book was designed to teach you everything you need to know in order to escape the typical life of dysfunction, self-destruction, lack, and defeat—and begin a new journey toward acquiring everything

God has for you. This includes joy, happiness, purpose, fulfillment, and peace from above, which surpasses all understanding
(Philippians 4:7).

Please note that this list mentions **nothing** about money and
earthly possessions. Don't get me wrong, there's nothing wrong
with being financially blessed, but that's not where happiness and
fulfillment come from. The truth is, even rich people find themselves in darkness at times. Many of them are trying to figure this
thing out like the rest of the world.

With so many different ideas, philosophies, and opinions of
the so-called "truth" to choose from, it's no wonder everyone is so
confused. I most definitely used to be one of them, until I discovered the *master key* to life.

It wasn't until I got fed up with the dysfunction of life and
the dysfunction within myself, that I threw my hands up and said,
"I give up. God, you win."

I used to think I was a "learn from your mistakes" kind of
person. However, there were things I fervently told myself I would
never do again. Yet, I found myself doing those very
things…again. *Haven't I already learned this lesson?* I thought, truly
perturbed and scratching my head.

What was wrong with me?

I didn't know then, but I know now—and we will get to that,
because if there's anything in the world that we need to understand, it's ourselves.

When I realized I couldn't actually depend on me, my own
knowledge, my own might, and my own will, I knew it was time
to do something different. Because, in reality, I *should* be able to
depend on me. If I can't depend on myself to do better—me being

the one who is immediately and directly affected by the things that I do, the one who has to live with every decision I make—then, who can I depend on?

If not me…then who?

At that very moment, only one answer came to mind: *God.*

Hmmm. Makes sense, I thought.

Besides God, who else can we depend on to save us from this world and from ourselves? When we get tired of trying and failing, when we get tired of getting it wrong, when we get sick and tired of being sick and tired, where do we turn? One thing I did know was that it needed to be something different, something positive, and something effective—because nine times out of ten, humans turn to distractions, not solutions.

Been there, done that.

My next step suddenly seemed so clear.

At this point all I wanted to know was what God wanted and what *He* put me on this earth to do. *What else really matters when this life is over?* I thought.

I made a decision, New Year's Day 2020, to give my life completely to God and never look back. I needed to do something different because, after all, to get something you've never had before, you have to do something you've never done before.

The one thing I had not done in my life was trust God 100 percent and do EVERYTHING He tells me to.

I gave up on trying to do things my way because I had done that my whole life. It wasn't working. I soon realized that anything God recommends, or commands rather, were things I wish I actually could do and be. I noticed that everything God promotes and condones is actually good for me and, by leaps and bounds, would get me closer to being the person I always wanted to be and living the life that I truly wanted to live—a happy, peaceful, and fulfilling one.

If we really think about it, we know that if we actually had the audacity to obey God, our lives would inevitably be better.

For example, humans love and admire truly good and honest people. Many people wish they could be honest. God commands us to be honest and not lie. Most people can't stand self-righteous, arrogant people. We love humble and kind people. That's everything Jesus is, everything God promotes, and everything God commands us to be. Get it?

Our Creator and Heavenly Father commands us to be our best selves, which is the same thing that most of us want and strive for. Most people get turned off when they hear the word *command*, but when you look at it from the proper perspective, you can see the love in it and how it only benefits, enhances, and protects us.

God is infinite in wisdom. There's no way we can always grasp or understand everything He tells us to do and why, but we usually always find out why certain things are good or bad for us eventually. The thing is, we can learn the easy way or the hard way. It's a choice.

The one thing I had never done was fully obey God and give myself and my life 100 percent to Him. And so...the decision was made.

I made one decision, and one decision changed *everything*. Because of this decision, I have clarity, answers, happiness, fulfillment, and the list goes on. I never knew life could be this way.

This decision turned me into a published author when I didn't even know I was a writer. Before, I didn't know who I really was and what I was capable of. This life is waiting for each and every one of us, but it doesn't come by doing things our way. This, we know from experience.

I'm sharing with you exactly what I did, what I do, how I think, and how I live my life. I'm sharing one solution with you that has been proven by all who dared to follow the road less traveled. Everyone I know who lives by the concepts written in this book have all acquired the same unprecedented results, myself included.

I listen to one voice and one voice only. *That* is how I discovered what everyone has been searching for—and I'm so happy that I can finally say, "I get it now." I felt it was my duty to share my story, my experience, and all I have learned to reach a place that so many dream of and even more assume can't be attained. If you feel you are nothing like the majority of this world or you're trying to find a way to get out of the "normal" dysfunctional lifestyle that most human beings settle for, this book is for you.

You have questions. So…where do you go when you need reliable answers?

As for me, I went directly to the Source. My answers and clarity came from indulging in God and His Word, The Living Bible, instead of remaining in patterns and cycles that were destroying me.

This book was written to provide you with wisdom, insight, perspective, and food for thought that will change your life and get you past the hurdles, barriers, thoughts, patterns, and behaviors that have been holding you back from experiencing life as God intended.

This book is designed to help you get out of your own way and get to the root of the everyday issues you face. If you want a better you, if you want a better way, and if you want a better life—this book is for you—and if you already have all the answers then why did you pick up this book? Just kidding—this book is for you too! No matter where you are in life, this book is bound to equip you with more—more knowledge, more wisdom, and more understanding. This book is configured so that *anyone* can learn from it—whether young or mature in faith.

There is A LOT of powerful information within the pages of these chapters. I recommend that you get your highlighter or favorite note-taking mechanism ready because you'll want to be able to quickly and easily refer back to any impactful information that will help get you to where you're trying to go in life.

I've included an "End-of-Chapter Reflection" exercise and note-taking section at the end of each chapter for an enhanced learning experience. You can find and download the free fillable and printable PDF version at: www.LatinaNicholeSmith.com/free.

Finally, if you really want answers to life's most plaguing questions and if you truly want to see a change in your life, be sure to read this book in its entirety—more than once even. No matter how far you've read, it will continue to surprise you. When reading, if you feel you have a question that hasn't been answered, you likely haven't gotten to that part yet.

You *will* walk away with a deep and solid understanding of God, life, people, and yourself after reading this book. Correspondingly, be sure to read the book completely, as every chapter builds upon itself and brings everything together full circle.

It is my deepest desire, hope, and prayer that every word in this book fills you with love, clarity, peace, healing, excitement, direction, answers, transformation, and everything you've been needing and hoping for.

My mission is to not only let it be known that you *can* break the cycle of dysfunction and escape such madness, but also *how*. So without further ado, let's jump right in and talk about the very thing everyone wants to know: why life sucks and how to fix it!

Chapter 1

Why Life Sucks For So Many

There are a number of reasons life sucks for so many, and in this book, we will cover them all. Sometimes things happen that are beyond our control. However, we have a lot more control over the quality of our lives than we give ourselves credit for, and this is where I'd like to start.

Most people go half, most, or all of their lives living in dysfunction. They keep doing the same things and following the same patterns and behaviors as the world. They partake in the same dysfunctional and self-destructive behaviors, even though this has only kept them in a never-ending cycle of dissatisfaction, pain, and misery.

Life doesn't have to be this way.

I heard an interesting story once and it really stuck with me. There were two brothers who grew up in the same household.

A friend asked the first brother, "How come you don't drink?"

"My father was an alcoholic," he replied.

The friend then asked the second brother, "Why are you an alcoholic?"

"*My father was an alcoholic,*" he answered.

Interesting. Two people, same experience, different outcomes. Now, when it comes to escaping dysfunction and the pursuit of happiness, which brother would you say "gets it"?

Right. The answer is brother number one. The one who *chose* to be different. The one who saw toxic, self-destructive behavior, which likely adversely affected his family, and decided, "I want to be *nothing* like that. I WILL be nothing like that."

The answer was simple, and it's as simple in life as it is on paper. All it takes to find yourself closer to happiness is having the proper perspective—and that's what you will have after reading this book.

As a human being, it's important to abandon the victim mentality displayed by the second brother. That way of thinking creates a domino effect in our lives. The truth is, you have the power to choose who you will be. You can allow unfavorable circumstances to make you worse, for a depressing future—or to make you better, for a brighter future. You can choose to be *exactly* like the defective people you encounter in life, or you can decide to be *nothing* like them.

From the sidelines, we can clearly see the downside of being like the defective people we encounter, however that is a normal choice that many humans make. If you *choose* to emulate bad behavior, it is highly likely that life will suck for you.

The beautiful thing about life is, at any moment, we can change the kind of choices we make. It's never too late.

*"The only person you are destined to become
is the person you decide to be."*
- Ralph Waldo Emerson

There's another common phrase: "If you can't beat 'em, join 'em." Many people follow this motto. However, following such a motto is catastrophic when it comes to mimicking, behaving, and thinking in toxic, unkind, and self-destructive ways.

This leads me to another common occurrence and example. We all know a person who was lied to or hurt by someone they really loved and trusted. There are cases when the person who was hurt decides that from now on, they will be the heartbreaker. They decide they will show no loyalty to anyone and will essentially do the same thing to others that was done to them. I call this person: the heartbroken heartbreaker.

The problem with this type of response is, you let a teachable moment take you down a dark rabbit hole. Your offender tried to bring you down, and you made sure they did by becoming just like them. You hated that person because they were a lying, no good piece of _____, and then you became them. Now, what do you think will happen next? You'll end up feeling the same way about yourself that you felt about them. If you don't like yourself and if you are acting out of hate and bitterness, you're now at the place where self-destruction and self-sabotage begins. It's never worth it.

*"Always choose righteousness, no matter what others do. If
they hurt you, don't take vengeance. Stay kind and move on.
They make their own karma; don't let them dictate yours."*
- Latina Nichole Smith

Because of this follow-the-crowd mentality, most people aren't living the kind of life they actually want to be living. Many people in the world are miserable, lost, empty, lonely, and feel unfulfilled in life, including in their jobs and relationships. They have no idea what to actually believe in or which way to go.

If this is the world as we know it, why *choose* to do what everyone else is doing? Especially when it's clear that doing what everyone else is doing will leave you no better off than they are. Even worse, why take advice and direction from them? That's what you call "the blind leading the blind" *(Luke 6:39)*.

So, when it comes to mankind, a major cause of our dysfunction is not solely due to the trials we encounter in life, but how we respond to them. Another cause is not giving proper consideration to our own actions and how greatly they determine the experiences we encounter.

So what is the answer, the cure, the solution?

It all starts with one superhuman God-given attribute, and our willingness to desire it, capture it, and cultivate it every day:

Wisdom

Wisdom is the key to escaping, and even bypassing, many of the problems we face in life. Now you can probably see why God tells us throughout His Word that above all, we are to seek wisdom *(Proverbs 4:5-19)*. Although the entire Bible consists of wisdom, the book of Proverbs is specifically dedicated toward the teaching of wisdom. Making good decisions and choices is everything, and in the end, it's the only difference between those who navigate life triumphantly and those who don't. Poor decision-making is a problem for many people and it often results in unfavorable out-comes in our lives. That's why we need to tackle this first and foremost. <u>Good decision-making is evidence of wisdom.</u>

> *"Happy is the person who finds wisdom,*
> *and the one who gets understanding.*
> *For wisdom is more profitable than silver,*
> *and her gain is better than fine gold.*
> *She is more precious than jewels,*
> *and nothing you desire can compare with her."*
> *Proverbs 3:13-15*

So, how do we gain wisdom and where do we even begin?

Reverence for the Lord is the beginning of wisdom *(Proverbs 9:10)*. The good news is, He gives it freely to anyone who asks *(James 1:5)*. In order to grow in wisdom and acquire the ability to make good, prosperous, and fulfilling choices, one must under-stand the difference between good and bad, right and wrong, love and hate, good and evil…you get the point.

The Bible is where wisdom resides. We've all heard the fa-mous saying, "What goes around comes around." No truer statement exists. This paraphrased dose of wisdom originates from the Bible, as does all useful self-help advice that can be found on the lips of wise men. The Bible version of this phrase is found in *Galatians 6:7* and tells us that, *"A man reaps what he sows."* Let's dissect this a bit.

Reap means to harvest or receive. *Sow* means to disseminate or plant. This analogy has to do with planting seeds. So, in other words, what you put out comes back to you. If you plant bad or wrongdoings, this will come back and manifest in your life experiences—and vice versa, if you plant good and right doings, this will bring favor and good things into your life.

So, if you truly want a good life, before you *do* anything, you must ask yourself this question—will this cause bad or good to manifest in my life? Then, make the decision, and live with the consequences. Good or bad, the choice is yours. You don't have to sit around and let life happen to you. You have a God-given right to *choose* your own destiny. It's called free will. The choices you make today determine your tomorrow.

Now, it's true we can't always choose whether or not hard times come, but we can always choose how we will respond when they do.

So, how do we differentiate between good and bad? This may seem simple, but I'm going back to the basics because this is a concept that's often disregarded, but it must be understood: If it's something you wouldn't want done to you, then it can safely be categorized as bad. For example, would you like to be lied to? Would you like to be falsely accused? Would you like it if someone stole from you or murdered someone you love? If you made a mistake, would you like it if your loved one never forgave you? Would you like it if you needed help and no one was there to help you? Would you like it if you had kids and they disobeyed and disrespected you when everything you did for them was out of love? Would you like it if your spouse cheated on you?

I am guessing the answer is no.

Many of the questions I just asked here stem from...can you guess? The Ten Commandments *(Exodus 20:2-17)*.

What I'm about to say next, I'm saying from experience. If you allow the Ten Commandments to be the moral compass that shapes your core values, and if you decide to faithfully follow and live by these principles, your life will be exponentially better. Even when life doesn't go your way, it will still be distinguishably set apart from the type of life that most people experience. The reason for this is because the Ten Commandments teach us exactly how to *love* and *respect* God, ourselves, and others. They teach us how to plant good seeds and they literally keep us from planting bad ones. Obedience is "The Special Sauce." We talk more about this in Chapter 7.

The only type of person who would answer yes to the aforementioned questions would be someone who delights in evil. Those individuals have a conscious or unconscious desire to live lives of torture, darkness, destruction, unfulfillment, repeated failure, and turmoil. Anything that is the opposite of good will *never* flourish or prosper; not indefinitely. This goes against the laws of nature.

When it comes to unrighteous gains, it isn't a matter of *if* it will all come crashing down. It's a matter of *when*.

Simply put, intentionally doing wrong is a waste of time. It's like spending all of your time and effort acquiring or building something wonderful just so you can lose it at some point in the future.

> *"Doing what one knows is* **NOT RIGHT**
> *often presents the illusion that he is winning,*
> *when in reality, he is* **LOSING.**

*Doing that which is **RIGHT**
sometimes presents the illusion that one is losing,
when in reality, he is **WINNING**."
- Latina Nichole Smith*

So, the answer to the question of why life sucks for so many is simply because most people do not *follow* or *obey* God's wise counsel about life and the things we should do as human beings. If a person created a thing, wouldn't you go to that person to find out how it works? Especially if that thing seems to be malfunctioning?

If a car malfunctions, you go to a mechanic. If your electrical outlets don't work, you call an electrician. If you're getting bad grades, you call a tutor. But when it comes to ourselves as human beings, when we begin to malfunction, we will go to everyone and everything for a solution besides the *One* who *knows*. Human beings will try everything else before looking to God, our Creator, if they even look to Him at all.

Separation from God is the root cause of darkness, and it's the root cause of feeling lonely, feeling lost, feeling unhappy, feeling confused, and feeling life sucks.

When problems arise, people often turn to drugs, alcohol, jobs, clothes, people, relationships, sex, exercise, and the list goes on. The number of things that people turn to first is astronomical, none of which get to the root of the issues we face. In fact, quite the opposite. Most of these are temporary distractions which only add fuel to what started out as a small flame.

God tells us *exactly* how to function optimally as human beings in this world, but how many people do you know who actually *listen* to God and *obey* His commands? Few. It's easy to see where humans have been getting it wrong. The world keeps going further and further away from God. You've probably noticed. The question is, will you continue to follow it?

God does *not* give us commandments so life will suck. God gives us commandments so life WON'T suck! Understand this simple concept, embrace it, and your life will never be the same. You will become a part of the select few who "get it" and life will NOT suck for you. It won't be perfect. There is no such thing. But it definitely will not suck.

If you would like a great example, read the entire story of Joseph in Genesis chapters 37-50. I absolutely believe everyone should read this story! It will show you what life looks like when you stay on the right path, regardless of your circumstances.

I was reading the Bible one day, and it stated that, back in the days before the flood, Noah was the ONLY righteous man in existence during his time *(Genesis 6:8-9)*.

Can you imagine that? You probably can because most people, even today, feel there are no truly good and genuine people in the world. This statement isn't 100 percent true, but it certainly is easy to make that assumption given the unfavorable behavior of the masses.

At any rate, this explains why life sucks for most. Instead of thinking about the things that God instructs us to do and how these things benefit and help us, most choose to rebel, disregard, and do just the opposite.

It seems people would rather focus on things about God that we don't understand, the things that can't help us, and the things that don't make a difference, rather than focusing on the things that we *do* understand, that *can* help us, and that *do* make a difference. Read that again! We'll talk more about that in Chapter 5.

All throughout the Bible, God tells us *exactly* what to do and what *not* to do in order to have a good, fulfilled, and prosperous life. That's the point of His instruction and guidance.

Why would our Creator create us and place us in this world without telling us how to live, win, lose, and navigate in this thing called life? The answer is, He didn't. Everything we need to know about life, and I do mean EVERYTHING, can be and is found in the Bible through direct instruction and examples.

As you continue reading this book, you will see in detail through the use of everyday examples, how I correlate biblical principles to the facts of life and how the information I have compiled substantiates itself.

As you navigate through the chapters, you will have the opportunity to see how every component ties together. Remember to read each chapter so you can be one of the few who are no longer confused about God, life, people, or yourself!

Now, let's move on to the next chapter and talk in detail about the one thing that everybody wants to know and needs to understand!

End-of-Chapter Reflection

Chapter 1
Why Life Sucks *For So Many*

You may download the fillable and printable PDF version at:
www.LatinaNicholeSmith.com/free

1. Name one or more reasons life sucks for so many?

_____

_____

_____

_____

_____

_____

_____

_____

2. Name one or two key elements to unsucking your life? (One word each)

_____

3. What are your biggest takeaways from Chapter 1?

_____

_____

_____

_____

_____

_____

_____

_____

_____

4. How will you incorporate what you learned from Chapter 1 into your life today (and moving forward)?

_____

_____

_____

_____

_____

_____

_____

_____

_____

_____

5. Name something new that you discovered about yourself (if applicable).

_____

_____

_____

_____

_____

_____

_____

_____

_____

_____

6. Name something new or interesting that you learned about God, life, and/or mankind.

_____

_____

_____

_____

_____

_____

_____

7. Journal any other notes, takeaways, or reminders that you'd like to capture from Chapter 1.

_____

_____

_____

_____

_____

_____

_____

Chapter 2

The Purpose of Life
Part One

Here we are, the big question! What is the purpose of life? This is one of the most important questions we could ever ask as human beings. Not only is it important for us to ask this question, it's critical for us to know the answer, and here's why.

When you understand why you were created and why you are here, it makes life a lot easier to navigate, understand, and enjoy. It alleviates unnecessary worry and confusion. It promotes a sense of peace, power, and stability within. This luxury is obtained when you understand the importance of going to the Source of truth for answers and actually *applying* the knowledge you obtain. That's exactly what wisdom is.

When it comes to the purpose of life, there are many philosophies. So, how do you know which one is the truth? Well, one philosophy that does not seem plausible to me is that there is no purpose. The thought of that, in my opinion, is depressing in itself. Everything has a purpose, whether we know its purpose or not. Just because we don't understand why or how something happened or was created doesn't mean it happened or was created for no reason.

Many people are dissatisfied in life because they didn't get the job, car, house, guy, or girl they wanted. The list goes on and on when it comes to the things we expect and hope for in life; but the bottom line is, life here on Earth is *not* about us. Once you're able to grasp this truthful reality, life becomes much easier to understand, tolerate, and navigate. Life is *not* about what WE want! Many people are lost, upset, or disgruntled because they expect things that God never promised us and that have nothing to do with the reason we were created and placed in the world to begin with.

Think about it. We often get mad when times get hard and when things don't go our way, but we were not put here to fulfill *our* own plan. God put us here to fulfill *His* plan. It isn't about you. It isn't about me. It's about God's plan. God's wisdom supersedes ours. So naturally, His plan is beyond human comprehension.

The blueprint God provided us, which is the Bible, informs us that He created each one of us for a specific reason and to carry out specific tasks in the world *(John 9:4, Romans 12:4-8)*. Therefore, your life has meaning. Your life has a purpose. The closer you are to God, the closer you are to fulfilling that purpose and the happier you will be because you will then be doing what you were designed to do instead of what you were not, which only results in dysfunction and unfulfillment.

The Bible tells us in *John 16:33* that we will have trials in this world but that we shouldn't worry. God is in complete control.

All we have to do is *trust* and *obey,* and He will take care of the rest. Peace comes when we realize this truth and stop worrying and trying so hard to control everything ourselves.

You gain peace from knowing God and His Word, and it mentally prepares you for anything you may face in life. This is why it's so important to know God and to read the Bible for yourself. With every word, you are getting closer and closer to discovering what God created you for. I'm telling you this from experience. Only the One who put you in this world can tell you why. Of course you will be lost and confused if you are looking and learning from the wrong places. The Bible is so divine because God speaks to each of us individually through His Word, giving us the guidance and direction we need in order to fulfill the purpose He called us to.

The Bible is literally the instruction manual for life. With that in mind, how can you function optimally if you have never taken the time to read through it *completely* and apply it as you go in life? We will talk more about this in Chapter 6. For now, let's go into more detail about the purpose of life.

The reason we were created can be summed up with *one* word:

Love

We were created to love. The only thing in existence that truly matters is love. You may have heard this statement before, but we need to go deeper and put this into perspective. To really understand and apply what I just said, we must know what love actually is. Believe it or not, there are many people in the world who don't know what love is or how to love. Sadly, society is more familiar with fake love than real love. Fake love is pretty much the opposite of God's definition of love. The Bible clearly tells us what love *is* and what it is *not*:

> *"Love is patient, love is kind. It does not envy, it does not boast, it is not proud. It does not dishonor others, it is not self-seeking, it is not easily angered, it keeps no record of wrongs. Love does not delight in evil but rejoices with the truth. It always protects, always believes, always hopes, always perseveres. Love never fails..."*
> 1 Corinthians 13:4-8

1 Corinthians 13 and *1 Corinthians 14:1* tells us the true definition of love and how love is to be our greatest aim. If you actually believe you love someone, look at the biblical—true—definition of the word and then ask yourself, do you really show or feel true love for this person(s)?

When you put love at the forefront of everything you do, you will not lose. You will not fail. Love never fails. God is love *(1 John 4:7-8, 1 John 4:16)*. In the previous chapter, we learned that, in doing what's right, you may have the illusion, at times, that you are losing or failing when in reality, you are winning. Love works the same way. If you put love and kindness on the back burner, you may at times have the illusion that you are winning, when you are actually losing. Which, again, is a choice.

Now, let's go even deeper. We were created to love. So, what happens when we don't do what we were designed and created to do? Before we answer this, I would like to pose this question again:

Who creates something of significance but doesn't provide guidance or instructions for that creation to function optimally? No one. Everything operationally complex and significant in this world comes with an instruction manual. Thankfully, this includes life as well.

If we look at the things that go on in the world today, we can see that an astounding number of human beings are operating dysfunctionally. More often than not, there are things we know are not good for us, yet we keep doing them *(Romans 7:15)*. Is that not dysfunctional? We've all been there!

But why is the world, and most of the people in it, dysfunctional? Well, think of this. How many humans do you know who actually do what we were created to do, which is to love? Furthermore, how many people actually read and follow the instruction manual for life that was provided to us by the Creator Himself? Close to zero, right? Again, it's no wonder why people feel life sucks.

Take this for example. A car was made for a reason, which is to travel and maneuver on land. If you take a car and try to drive it onto the beach and a mile into the ocean, what will happen? It will malfunction because that is not what it was created for. Likewise, a boat was designed to travel through water. If you try to navigate a boat on dry land, it will suck. It's easy to see, in these scenarios, how operating a creation for something outside of what it was designed for leads to dysfunction.

Again, the Bible tells us everything we need to know about life and also gives us instructions on how to live and function optimally. The problem is, most don't follow it or even know what it says.

You were created for a reason. God created you because there was something broken or lacking in the world that your unique contribution and special gifts can speak to. Many people don't ever realize this. Therefore, they go through life feeling depressed, lost, and unfulfilled. Many of these things that God created us to do are not being done, leaving the world in distress and chaos.

Here is an example. We learned that everything God asks of us boils down to one thing: love one another *(Galatians 5:14)*. Imagine if everyone actually obeyed God's instruction! What if someone was poor or in need and we listened to God and helped them? Imagine if you were poor or in need and people willingly helped you just because God said so and because it's what we were created to do. *Love.*

Imagine if everyone was humble, kind, and loving to one another. Imagine if people cared more about people than money. I could go on and on. How much better would the world be? How much easier and more pleasant would life be? How much more sense would things make if people actually followed the operating manual for life, which the Creator left for us to follow in order to thrive and prevail as human beings in this world?

In the next chapter, we are going to jump into the second part of our purpose in existence! What's really going on in the world?

End-of-Chapter Reflection

Chapter 2
The Purpose of Life Part One

1. What is the purpose of life and what were we created to do? In other words, *who* and *what* is life all about?

_____

_____

_____

_____

_____

2. What are your biggest takeaways from Chapter 2?

_____

_____

_____

_____

_____

_____

_____

3. How will you incorporate what you learned from Chapter 2 into your life today (and moving forward)?

_____

_____

_____

_____

_____

_____

_____

4. Name something new that you discovered about yourself (if applicable).

_____

_____

_____

_____

_____

_____

5. Name something new or interesting that you learned about God, life, and/or people.

_____

_____

_____

_____

_____

_____

6. Journal any other notes, takeaways, or reminders that you'd like to capture from Chapter 2.

_____

_____

_____

_____

_____

_____

_____

Chapter 3

The Purpose of Life
Part Two

This Means War

In the previous chapter, we learned that we were designed and created to love. However, there's another integral aspect of our existence that we *must* be aware of.

One of the biggest battles we face in life is dealing with people because, more often than not, people don't choose to do the right thing, to love others, or to be kind. Some of the greatest pain and heartbreak we've faced has been at the hands of another human being. "Hurt people" hurt people, right? When does that cycle end? Our biggest battle is with people, yes—but on a deeper level, it's with the spirit that is operating behind the person. Our biggest battle is with people because people are the primary vehicle the devil uses in order to cause pain, destruction, and corruption in the world and in our lives.

Some people have knowingly and willingly switched sides and have no problem being used, abused, manipulated, and controlled by the devil. Others are more like sleepwalking and don't know what's really going on. They think it's "just them" or "just life"; however, there's more to it than that.

The answer to the question of what's really going on in the world is that there is a war taking place between good and evil. This battle is also known as spiritual warfare.

"So then, let us not be like others, who are asleep,
but let us be awake and sober."
1 Thessalonians 5:6 NIV

"For we wrestle not against flesh and blood, but against
principalities, against powers, against the rulers of the darkness
of this world, against spiritual wickedness in high places."
Ephesians 6:12 KJV

This scripture assures us of what the real battle is and who we are truly up against in this world. Whether we know it or not, we have chosen a side through our actions, and this directly impacts the quality and outcome of our lives. But, interestingly enough, this is a fixed fight. We already know which side wins in the end *(1 John 4:4)*.

You were placed in this temporary world with a higher calling and purpose—to be a soldier who fights against evil and darkness. But what's interesting, what's important, and what most don't understand is that the weapon we are to use against our enemy in this war is love. Remember, it's all about *love*. If we are relying on God to help us, we are relying on love because God is love, and love never fails. When we have God, we are backed by the highest power.

> *"The weapons we fight with are not the weapons*
> *of the world. On the contrary,*
> *they have divine power to demolish strongholds."*
> *2 Corinthians 10:4 NIV*

So, when you do what you were created to do, which is to love, you will have the power of God within and surrounding you, and you will *not* lose this war. A big part of why God says there will be trials in the world is because the adversary (devil, satan, evil forces) will always be strategically plotting to bring you down. But the adversary has no power unless you give it to him. That isn't a typo, by the way. That name doesn't get a capital letter in my book.

> *"I have given you power and authority to trample on snakes*
> *and scorpions and over all the power of the enemy, and*
> *nothing shall by any means hurt you."*
> *Luke 10:19*

The devil strategically uses people, relationships, and disappointments in life to steal your faith and take you out of the powerful purpose God has called you to. Those are the types of weapons the enemy uses. If he can cause you to get angry with God and cause you to hate people, then he has accomplished his goal. He has succeeded at taking you down with him.

*"Be sober, be vigilant; because **your adversary** the devil walks*
about like a roaring lion, seeking whom he may devour."
1 Peter 5:8 NKJV

A perfect example of this is the scenario we saw in Chapter 1 with the heartbroken heartbreaker. As we know, you were created for a purpose. The adversary succeeds when he can distract you or keep you from fulfilling it. The devil has children (demons and demonettes) working for him. We know this in reality when we see people who are not only intentional, but totally content hurting others.

We also know that the devil is the father of lies *(John 8:44)*, and he is very persuasive and deceitful. We've all come across one of these types, or perhaps someday we will. Like a sucker, I've fallen for a trap or two set by the devil, but I'm more than ecstatic to say I know better now. I hope you're ready to wake up, come alive, and exercise the power you have over the enemy because that is exactly what this type of wisdom equips you to do!

Because demons are spirits, they have to work through people just like the almighty Holy Spirit works through us when we become Christians. We invite Jesus and the Holy Spirit to come in and take over; we relinquish control to God. Well, this applies to those who understand what being a Christian really means. We discuss this in Chapter 9. Just a quick side note, God is a gentle soul. He is the opposite of the devil. God does not force Himself on us. He waits for us to invite Him in. The devil, however, does not respect boundaries, and he doesn't ask you for control. He takes it and keeps taking it as long as you allow him to. When we are too far from God—living in sin and disobedience—this gives the devil easy access to defeat us and use us to destroy ourselves and others. We have to pay attention to people's behavior so we can know who sent them. This is called discernment. We talk about this in Chapter 8. As you can see, or will soon see, I'm not cutting any corners when it comes to preparing you to trample on snakes and walk victoriously through this dark world shining like the light that you are and were created to be! I'm here for it.

Speaking of being prepared, I highly recommend educating yourself on a topic that people are becoming more aware of: *Narcissism*. If you study this "disorder" (Narcissistic Personality Disorder, or NPD) from a spiritual standpoint, you will understand the extreme necessity of educating yourself on these types of people. Knowing how they act and knowing their tricks and traits will save you loads of heartache, pain, stress, depression, and wasted time.

Narcissists are the most toxic types of people. Some are overt, or easily identifiable, but the coverts are the most dangerous. They are undetectable to the untrained eye; wolves in sheep's clothing. They cause extreme amounts of mental, psychological, spiritual, and sometimes physical damage.

Have you ever looked at a person's relationship and wondered, *why in the world are they still with this monster?* Causing pain is one of their specialties and because of the strong influence they have over their prey, it would behoove you to never get caught up with one to begin with.

I won't go into great detail on narcissism in this book, but it's a very important matter to at least introduce. Because we have to interact with people on a regular basis, and because narcs often show up looking like everything we've ever wanted, it's easy to get tied up with one. If you don't like the term *narcissist*, you can alternatively research "toxic people" and learn their traits, as well as how to identify them, and how to handle them.

When you begin learning about narcissistic people, you may question yourself and wonder if you might be the toxic one. This is normal, especially if you've ever dealt with this type. They are very good at making you feel like there is something wrong with you, and they often bring out the worst in us.

If you do happen to notice that you have toxic traits, don't be discouraged. Learning about toxic people is dually beneficial. Not only does it help us learn what to stay away from, but it's a healthy way for us to identify if we have any traits that we need to work on or eliminate. It's a great way to discover if or where we need healing. You will understand more and more as you learn about it.

Once you learn who narcissists are and how they operate, they will end up losing control over you and will lose their ability to mislead, frustrate, influence, and upset you. That's just what they do.

Just like a basketball coach selects certain opponents for each of his players to "stay on" in the game, the devil attempts to assign and attach demons to each of us. They're not scary zombies like we see on television. They blend in as they intend. They know our weaknesses, they know what we love, and through conversation or observation, they know what we've been missing. They will give you an overwhelming amount of what you want, as well as an overwhelming amount of what you *don't* want. They are parasitic, which is why identifying and keeping a distance is always the best route with these types. They're good at what they do, but when you are aware of the signs, they can be easily identified. They can and will take years of your life, peace, happiness, and purpose away if you aren't aware of what you're dealing with. You may be wondering how I know. Well…that's another book altogether!

The Bible gives several examples of how the enemy uses typical life circumstances against us. Knowing God's Word helps keep you steps ahead of the enemy because you will have an understanding of the tricks he uses in an attempt to bring you down.

Since God has created us and called us to fight alongside Him in this war against evil, He is the only One who can lead us into our purpose triumphantly. For this reason, it's important to understand how vital it is to stay close to God, connected to God, and in His presence daily. This is accomplished through regular prayer, reading scripture, and *obedience*. This is our weapon and shield against the kingdom of darkness.

The devil's goal is to separate you from God because he knows that he *cannot* defeat God. The devil knows that when you walk with God—the stronger your relationship with God and the closer you are to God—the less power he has over you. If the devil can separate you from God, he can lead you into addiction, he can lead you into self-destruction, he can lead you into depression, lack, dysfunction, and the like. So be careful when people are talking against God and just be mindful of who sent them.

Now that we know the root cause of misery, dysfunction, and lack for most people in the world—being disconnected from our Heavenly Father and His protective instruction—we must now understand and come to realize the necessity of staying close to God as well. It's important to realize we need God's Holy Spirit in our lives just as much, and even more than we need air, food, and water.

Some people think fellowship with God once a week or once a year will do. But do we eat once a year or once a week? No, because we would literally die or, at a minimum, we would be unable to function properly. So, if you're tired of feeling defeated, unhappy, confused, and unfulfilled, it's time to step away from the world's approach and view of life and God.

You must understand that we need the Holy Spirit, food, water, *and* air DAILY in order to survive, thrive, live, prevail, and function properly.

So, we know what happens when we don't get water—dehydration. We know what happens when we don't get food—starvation. We know what happens when we don't get air—suffocation. Now, we know what happens when we don't spend time with God daily—defeat.

For human beings, going too long without consuming *any one* of these essential elements is a matter of life or death. Living in this world without God's continuous presence, guidance, and protection means being spiritually dead (unfulfilled, lost, and damned). Hence, life will suck, as it does for many.

We need the presence of God in our lives as much as we need the air that we breathe. Understanding this simple concept is the key to life.

The adversary is extremely crafty. He knows how to get into your head, confuse you, and trick you into doing self-destructive things by making them appear to be shiny, glorious, and fun. Most people regularly experience this. When you succumb to what your flesh wants instead of being led by the Spirit and wisdom of God, you begin to experience a mediocre existence. This is the adversary's goal and he has won many souls, as you may well know. When you are connected to your Creator and in His Word, you maintain wisdom and power over the enemy.

Life is an open-book test and we know where the answers are found. When it comes to the war between good and evil, we already know that wickedness never ultimately prevails over righteousness. We see this in television and movies. We see it in everyday life. It's always only a matter of time before the bad guy's world and plans all come crashing down.

It usually looks, for a short minute, like the bad guy is winning and like the good guy is losing; but, before it's all over, the good guy prevails, and in reality, he always will.

"For only good men enjoy life to the full; evil men
lose the good things they might have had…"
Proverbs 2:21-22 TLB

Ever notice in the movies how the good guy always tries to save the bad guy in the end, even after all of the wrong that was done toward him? This part used to seriously perturb me, but after getting closer to God, I understand why He commands us to love even our enemies.

The bad guy usually dies even though the good guy tries to save him, but sometimes he is saved and becomes so ashamed, astounded, and inspired by the goodness of the good guy that he turns from his evil ways *(1 Peter 3:16-17 TLB)*. That's why God commands us to always be kind and forgiving. We are to lead by example. It's about God's will. It's about spreading love and help-ing lost souls find their way out of dysfunction and back to God. Back to victory. Back to life.

Again, this spiritual war is a fixed fight. God will not lose. He is God and He is love. So, when you choose to walk with God, you are choosing to be on the winning team, which is what you were created to do. You were created to win.

When you choose to go throughout life succumbing to sin—having lustful and destructive values—you are consciously or sub-consciously placing yourself on a losing team. We all have free will to choose which path we will take.

We know the truth. God put the truth in our hearts *(Hebrews 10:16)*. The problem is, many people turn away from the truth when it doesn't fit the lifestyle *they* want to live. It's evident that when you choose to make your own rules and live your own way, you are entering the territory of operating outside of how you were created to operate, which breeds dysfunction.

Usually, what *we* want brings destruction upon ourselves, but what God wants us to do brings peace, protection, and prosperity *(Galatians 5:16-26)*. The reason for this is because, as children of God, we have very limited knowledge of life, what's ahead, and what we need compared to God's infinite knowledge and fore-sight.

It's no different from telling your small child to not jump into eight feet of water when they haven't learned how to swim yet. It looks amazing and fun to them, but you have more years of wis-dom, so you will stop them because you know it isn't safe; or you will go with them to keep them safe, and they will refer to you as a buzzkill or a party pooper. Every day, people jump into the dangerous waters of life without God, and they are drowning. This metaphor depicts the importance of staying close to God—your Creator and your Protector. It's a must to stay in His presence through prayer, obedience, and reading His Word.

I once heard a wise quote, "Change starts head first," which brings us to the next chapter.

End-of-Chapter Reflection

Chapter 3
The Purpose of Life Part Two
This Means War

1. What's really going on in the world, and what is the other reason we were created?

_____

_____

_____

_____

_____

2. What is our enemy's goal, and what happens if he accomplishes it?

_____

_____

_____

_____

_____

_____

3. What are your biggest takeaways from Chapter 3?

_____

_____

_____

_____

_____

_____

_____

_____

4. How will you incorporate what you learned from Chapter 3 into your life today (and moving forward)?

_____

_____

_____

_____

_____

_____

5. Name something new that you discovered about yourself (if applicable).

_____

_____

_____

_____

_____

_____

_____

6. Name something new or interesting that you learned about God, life, and/or mankind.

_____

_____

_____

_____

_____

_____

_____

7. Journal any other notes, takeaways, or reminders that you'd like to capture from Chapter 3.

_____

_____

_____

_____

_____

_____

_____

_____

_____

_____

_____

_____

_____

_____

_____

Chapter 4

Mental Essentials
Choice, Mindset, Perspective, Healing

Choice is Everything

W e've referenced the power of choice a few times. However, given the fact that choice plays such a significant role in our lives, I felt it only appropriate to park here for a moment and have a focused discussion on this important aspect. Everything starts with a choice. Therefore, choice really is everything.

When it comes time to make any decision (which is always), we must take Dr. Stephen R. Covey's approach and "*begin with the end in mind.*" It's important to always take that extra moment to think about our choices BEFORE we act on them because what's done is done. Acting without thinking is a recipe for disaster.

If you *choose* to be *pro*active and prevent bad choices and outcomes, you won't have to be sorry later. You won't have to try to clean up a mess you made or live with the bad circumstances of a poor, unthought-out decision. My mother always used to say, "Uh-oh is too late." It's okay if you aren't a pro at decision-making right now. Everything requires practice. The good news is, human beings, with consistent practice, we can master anything!

A person with the victim mentality blames everything on their circumstances. The truth is, we have more control than we'd like to admit! Choices are simple things that make all of the difference in your life. YOU decide what you will choose. Therefore, YOU decide how your life turns out, what you accomplish, and what you get out of life. **Start now by being conscious of your choices, the decisions you make, and where they lead you.**

You don't have to be old and wise to make good decisions. Here's the key. If you look ten steps ahead at a decision you are about to make, it's easy to have an idea of whether something good or bad will come from it. If you aren't certain, I would advise, if applicable, that you wait, be still, and talk to God about it before making the decision. Make sure you feel good about it within your soul and make sure you don't ignore red flags. Red flags are a great way to help formulate wise decisions. Ignoring red flags gets many of us into a lot of trouble. Been there, done that, got the t-shirt! Have you ever heard or said the words, "I should've known!" That usually translates to mean, "I saw the signs."

Being aware doesn't mean being fearful; it simply means being wise. Make good decisions—retrospectively—based on the data you have collected and likely outcomes. If you can foresee an outcome that you can't live with or don't want, then it may not be a situation worth jumping into! If you feel peace about it and you've prayed about it, then go ahead! If it still doesn't work out, learn whatever lesson is at hand and keep moving. Have peace with the fact that you did your part, and pay attention to whatever it is you needed to learn from that experience. It isn't a mistake if you learned from it. Mistakes are not the reason we give up; mistakes are the reason we grow.

A real-life example that I would like to use is this: Let's say you've met someone and you've been dating for a little while. You're trying to decide if you should trust this person, give them your heart, go all in, or whatever the case may be. Let's say you are hesitant for some reason. Maybe you've seen a couple of red flags. Maybe you have some "fear" about moving forward. First, you have to evaluate if this "fear" is valid, because sometimes it's easy for us to mistake wisdom for fear.

If you have a logical reason to be skeptical, then you should be. That is wisdom, not fear. In this case, you have more of a concern than fear. It's important to know the difference because "God has not given us the spirit of fear" *(2 Timothy 1:7)*. If you have seen red flags, can see yourself going down the same road you've been down before, or if you don't feel peace about a certain decision and you have a logical reason to pump the brakes, then do just that. Pay attention to that inner voice, and evaluate how you feel before making any decision that could lead you into a state of anxiety. You don't have to rush into trusting people. Take your time. Protect yourself and your heart. God warns us NOT to put our trust in man but only in Him *(Psalms 118:8)* and to guard our heart for it controls everything we do and determines the course of our lives *(Proverbs 4:23)*. Don't let anyone influence you otherwise. Trust your instincts. The closer we grow to God, the stronger we become, the wiser we become, and the less we have to worry about. Prioritizing our relationship with God is the *best* decision we will ever make.

Mindset and Perspective

Mindset, perspective, and choice are extremely determinative factors in our lives. Mindset and perspective, like choice, literally changes everything. If you want to see a positive change in your life, you have to change your mindset; meaning, the way you think and what you think about.

Remember the story from Chapter 1 about the two brothers? It's one of my favorites. This story is a great example to bring home the concepts discussed in this chapter.

Allow me to refresh your memory: There were two brothers who grew up in the same household. One brother was asked why he was an alcoholic. He replied, *"My father was an alcoholic."* The other brother was asked why he *doesn't* drink alcohol. His reply was *"My father was an alcoholic."* Interesting isn't it? Two people, same situation, different outcomes. So, if you have two people who have had the same negative environment and experiences, yet their lives turned out to be different, what made the difference?

The difference is mindset, perspective, and choice. One brother saw how damaging alcoholism is and decided he did *not* want to be like that, while the other decided he would go down the same road and blame his choices on his father's bad behavior. Was his father's behavior the problem? Or was it the fact that he decided to be just like his father? The point is, you have the power to determine your future, no matter what you've witnessed or been through.

You have to make a DECISION to love yourself and let tough times make you stronger, better, and smarter—not worse. Naturally, our minds often revert to thinking about things that bring us down. You have to train your mind to think about things that make you feel good. The truth is, we can think about or focus on things that make us feel better or we can think about things that make us feel like crap. That is why you hear people say happiness is a choice.

You don't have to let your mind think about whatever it wants. You can develop control over your mind and practice only thinking about things that make you feel good or positive actions you can take that will lift your spirit *(Philippians 4:8)*.

I read a book called *The Secret* by Rhonda Byrne. A statement from the book that really stood out to me was this: "Your feelings tell you, immediately, what you were thinking." Think about that for a moment. Powerful right?

The only time thinking about the negative is okay is if you are healing and examining the situation in order to see how you can be better, learn, and grow from it. That is necessary, but only in this case. We'll talk about healing in the next section. There is no other occasion, reason, or benefit to thinking about, focusing on, or dwelling on anything negative.

If you aren't mentally healthy right now, that's okay. You're not alone. Just decide, right away, to seek help to heal. There's nothing wrong with that! Just because you aren't mentally healthy now doesn't mean you can't ever be. We've all been there. Just never let your past determine or ruin your future. You can decide to leave dark days behind and to walk toward the light, better days, and better choices. Don't let a bad season or experience cause you to regularly make decisions that will only complicate your life and ruin your chances at a bright future.

It's never too late, and you're never too old to start making better decisions. Every good decision we make today leads to a better tomorrow.

Healing is Paramount

Another extremely important factor that too many people miss is the importance of healing. The first step to having a happy and whole life is healing from all past hurts. So many people go around every day living in dysfunction simply because they have not healed from past hurts. We have to heal in order to see and act clearly. Brokenness distorts our vision, our mindset, our choices, our actions, and our perspective, to say the least.

What does brokenness look like? Anger, bitterness, jealousy, envy, low self-esteem, insecurity, codependency, fear, and so forth. When we experience these types of feelings, we have to ask ourselves, "*Why? Where is this coming from?*" Get to the root of it and pull it out. Exactly and metaphorically.

This may not be the easiest stage to go through, but it *is* the most necessary. Pull the weed out by the roots. What most people do is cut the top, utilizing distractions or temporary fixes. We have to pull it out by the root so that it will not resurface in the form of triggers, toxicity, and self-sabotaging behaviors.

We've mentioned the popular expression, "hurt people" hurt people. Considering the fact that most of our heartache, pain, and disappointment stems from our interactions and involvement with other human beings, it's of the utmost importance that we all (every single human being on the planet) understand that we have to look within and heal ourselves first, before anything else, so that the cycle of "hurt people" hurting people can end, or at least begin to decline. Only then can we begin to experience the sweeter side of life as opposed to the dark side.

The wonderful thing about healing is, after you've gone through the healing process and have faced the issues that have been plaguing you, it doesn't hurt anymore. It no longer has control over you, your actions, and your feelings.

Let's take this for example: If you have a broken finger, it will hurt any time you move or touch it because it isn't healed. Once you see a doctor and put a cast on it, you've begun the healing process. When the healing process is over, you can bend and touch your finger *painlessly*. But if you stay away from the doctor and try to cover the pain with distractions (drugs, ice, homemade hand wrappings, and so on) every time you try to move it or touch it, it will hurt. It will be dysfunctional.

This is what most humans experience, so we end up easily triggered and controlled by past hurts that were never healed. Every reminder still hurts us and controls us and can even lead to a downward spiral and increased dysfunction in our lives.

Every human must begin, first and foremost, with self-work and self-reflection. As we can see from Michael Jackson's beautiful song, "Man in the Mirror," he tried to get the message out. It doesn't seem like many listened, which brings me to the core message of this book. We *have* to stop worrying about what other people are doing and look at ourselves and make a decision to do what WE know is right. We should not follow the masses and do what everyone else is doing.

We must be dedicated to the process of self-improvement as a lifestyle and connect with the select few who have made a decision to do the same. *This* is when our lives become different from the typical dysfunction that the majority experience.

"Do not be deceived: 'Bad company corrupts good character.'"
1 Corinthians 15:33 BSB

If you cannot find any of the select few, abandon any fear of being alone. Being alone is *not* a curse or a bad thing. It is peaceful. That's what it is. It's better to be solo and growing than to be in bad company and deteriorating. Plus, when you separate yourself from dysfunction, you will begin to attract what you are. That's the way it goes.

The Importance of the Proper Perspective

We *must* understand the importance of having the right perspective before we can even begin to unravel the most important questions in life. The Merriam-Webster dictionary defines perspective as "a mental view." So, perspective is how you see things. We believe in things based on how we view them mentally.

Therefore, your perception determines your faith (what you believe). If you believe something, you have faith in it, right? Seeing things the wrong way leads you to doing things the wrong way, consequentially rendering unfavorable results in life. When a person believes something, it is *their* truth. However, what we perceive and believe about life isn't always actually true. That's why it's important to always work on healing ourselves and seek wisdom from God to avoid being misguided or confused. Perceptions encompass your thoughts, thoughts lead to feelings, and feelings lead to actions.

THOUGHTS → FEELINGS → ACTIONS

Always remember this powerful statement and the importance of consciously directing your thoughts.

Now, we've determined that man's perception determines what he believes, which determines how he will act. So, if your belief system is wrong, your life goes wrong. Ever hear about elephants' fear of mice? But wait…how much bigger is an elephant than a mouse? And how much more damage can that elephant do to that mouse? As you can see here, the elephant doesn't react to a mouse based on reality; he reacts based on what *he* believes and what *he* perceives—*his* truth. *That* is the power of perspective. Faith (what you believe in) similarly determines the trajectory of your life and your actions.

For example, we either believe in God and His ways or we believe in the world and its way of doing things. Walking with God gives us good favor and lasting peace, even through adversity. Being of the world and following what everyone else does will get you what everyone else has: emptiness, fleeting joy, and no peace. This is precisely why God instructs us to be *in* the world but not *of* the world.

> *"And do not be conformed to this world,*
> *but be transformed by the renewing of your mind…"*
> Romans 12:2 NKJV

We must have the proper perspective because this determines our beliefs, which determine our actions, which determine our results. Getting the proper perspective begins with knowing the *truth* about life and how and where to find it.

There's only one perspective that matters and there's only one perspective that is true and good: God's perspective. Viewing and approaching the world through God's eyes will never lead you wrong.

Bonus

Besides The Living Bible (TLB), I've read some amazing books which have helped me develop and master the essential traits and characteristics mentioned in this chapter. I've created a free PDF list of these books, why I love them, and how they've helped me grow. You can download this freebie by visiting:

www.LatinaNicholeSmith.com/free

Next!

Many people find themselves asking the question, "Should we believe in God or not?" This is a very good question. Let's move on to the next chapter and talk about it!

End-of-Chapter Reflection
Chapter 4
Mental Essentials

1. What does brokenness look like?

_____

_____

_____

_____

_____

2. What are your biggest takeaways from Chapter 4?

_____

_____

_____

_____

_____

_____

_____

_____

3. How will you incorporate what you learned from Chapter 4 into your life today (and moving forward)?

_____

_____

_____

_____

_____

_____

_____

4. Name something new that you discovered about yourself (if applicable).

_____

_____

_____

_____

_____

_____

_____

_____

5. Name something new or interesting that you learned about God, life, and/or mankind.

_____

_____

_____

_____

_____

_____

_____

6. Journal any other notes, takeaways, or reminders that you'd like to capture from Chapter 4.

_____

_____

_____

_____

_____

_____

_____

Chapter 5

To Believe or Not to Believe?
That is the question.

O ne of the biggest queries of man is: Is there a God and should I believe in Him? Even some believers, at times, have found themselves asking themselves these very questions. This chapter is of utmost importance because this is easily the most consequential question *and* answer in human existence. It is "the question."

I understand how confusing and tantalizing it can be to cipher through so much critical information and have the responsibility of making the absolute best decision that will not only affect your life now, but your afterlife as well. Fortunately, the contents within this chapter are simple, to the point, and easy to follow.

When it comes to the question of whether or not God exists, the truth of the matter is, unbelievers say believers can't prove God exists and created the world. But they can't prove God doesn't exist or that He didn't create the world.

People can say many things, but no one can genuinely say that belief in God is unreasonable. The truth is, some people have made a decision to NOT believe. Therefore, no amount of evidence will ever convince them. I say this because, as long as humans have been in existence, no amount of proof or answers—regardless of how concrete they are—has stopped the same questions from circulating.

There are so many things science can't explain, yet many scientists and atheists will not give credit to God for any of them. People like this don't give God any credit because they simply don't want to, and odds are, they never will *(Jeremiah 6:10 NIV)*.

We can look at the sun, moon, stars, animals, and life in general. That's our proof *(Romans 1:20)*. Those are things human beings cannot create nor sustain. Scientists can only explore what God created and *try* to figure out how He did it. But if you need more proof, how many times have science and doctors said someone should be dead but they weren't? How many times have they said certain things aren't possible, but they happened anyway? How many times have miracles happened that went against the laws of nature? That was God. There's no other explanation, and yet, there are people who will argue against any and all of the above, even though there really is no other plausible answer.

"Denying the existence of Jesus doesn't make Him go away. It merely proves that no amount of evidence will convince you."
God's Not Dead 2

Some people already have their minds made up against God. Some people can't handle the idea that there's something out there greater than themselves—something that is more loving, complex, and intellectual than human beings can comprehend. They're entitled to believe whatever they want. We all are. But for anyone who may be on the fence, for anyone who may be swayed by these types of questions and ideas, and for anyone who really would like some information that can help solidify your faith and make sense of it all, this important context will help you clear the fog and more easily put it all into perspective.

When it comes to wrapping your mind around the concept of God, the key is NOT to examine the types of things no one can prove, but to examine the types of things we see everyday that 100 percent correlate with God's Word. *That* is what has determined and sealed my faith. And that's all I need in order to come to what I consider to be a wise, logical, and informed decision, which I have total peace with.

Too many people make the mistake of examining things that no one knows or understands and allowing those things to keep them trapped in confusion, stagnation, dysfunction, and lack. Instead, we should be paying attention to and focusing on the parts that we CAN see, apply, and observe, which is easily 90 percent of what the Bible says and we can see happening in everyday life.

I say this because when I made the decision to accept Jesus as my Lord and Savior and give my life to God, I decided I needed to know the Bible for myself. I wanted to know everything God said in His Word. I wanted to know everything He wanted us to know, and I wanted to know it for myself. Currently, I have read a little over half of the Bible, including the entire New Testament.

As I read and take notes every day, I've noticed that I have abundantly more answers than I do questions—and I understand more and more as I go.

What's interesting is that many people would rather focus on the small percentage of things in the Bible that they don't understand and can't prove, and base their beliefs on that, rather than focusing on the mounds of information that makes perfect sense.

The truth is, we will never understand everything in this world. Why do people expect to know and understand everything about God and the way life works if it's been determined by researchers that we are only capable of using a portion of our brain capacity? But they aren't sure of this. It's one thing one day and another the next, constantly changing. The only thing constant in the world is God and His Word (the Bible). For that reason, it's the only thing we can *always* rely on. The truth doesn't change. We talk more about this in the next chapter.

I don't understand details about how the telephone works. I don't understand how I can whisper into an object and someone on the other side of the Earth can hear me, clearly, in real-time. Early phones had two cans and a string, and you could see the person you spoke to from one tree house to another. Where is the string now? Is it floating on top of the Pacific Ocean? Did they dig underground beneath the seas for centuries to bury the line? Just sayin'. I don't understand everything about it, but I know it works, and I use it daily.

I don't understand how a heavy airplane flies through the sky or how a heavy boat doesn't sink, but I know one flies and one floats. I know there is someone out there capable of explaining the logistics of how these things work, just as I am here explaining

God, life, and mankind; however, I don't research those things because I don't need to know everything about everything. I just need to know enough. For some, enough is never enough.

At the end of the day, when it comes to anything in this life, either it works effectively or it doesn't. The only way to know if God's way works is to do it His way. Ninety-eight percent of people don't, and *that* is the root cause of dysfunction in this world.

Personally, I haven't found any explanations regarding life and things that happen in this world better than the answers that the Bible provides. In the previous chapter, we thoroughly discussed the importance of mindset and what we *choose* to believe in life. We have discussed how much this matters and how you receive what you believe.

So again, if a person believes there is no God and no validity to the Bible, that would mean there is no point to life. That would mean that we magically appeared in the world one day with no guidance, no instruction, and no help of any kind. We are just here today and gone tomorrow. Period. Again, that would mean life has no meaning and everything we do and go through is all for nothing. Hence, life sucks then you die.

If this is what a person chooses to believe, then this is true *for them*. Remember the elephants' example? What you believe becomes your reality.

"He who says he can
and he who says he cannot
are both correct."
- Confucious

This quote may seem a little off topic, but it's a great example of how our beliefs determine our reality. If a person believes there is no God or purpose for life, then this will be true, *for him*. This will be his reality. He will live a pointless and meaningless life, and it will be evident in his actions, experiences, and the quality of his life.

Furthermore, if a person believes in just the *idea* of "a higher power" but they don't know anything about that higher power, they have adopted a belief that provides no answers or direction. Therefore, they just wander aimlessly like a tumbleweed going in whatever direction the wind blows. That's instability. Not to mention, if they consider themselves a good and wise person, they are practicing the teachings and principles that come from a book they don't believe in—the Bible.

So, when it comes to things we can't know, but **are possible**, I've noticed that people will get insurance on their homes, just in case. People will get insurance on their car, just in case. People will get insurance on their cell phones, jewelry, and so on—just in case. "Just in case" something happens, they will be covered.

But when it comes to the most important thing in life—the eternal positioning of our soul—many people don't bother. We know with 100 percent certainty that there will come a day when we draw our last breath. No one knows when that day will come—and no one knows, *from experience* with 100 percent certainty what happens after we die. So, let's think about this for a moment. In this case, we know with **100 percent** certainty that we will die, but **0 percent** certainty what happens afterward. However, the majority of the planet gets insurance "just in case" on *everything* else but **0 percent** insurance in preparation for what *could* happen after life…"just in case." That's quite the gamble.

Many don't seem to care what happens to their soul when our temporary time is up here and have willingly opted NOT to be prepared for the unknown—even though this is easily the most consequential, irreversible, and damning decision of them all. For some, it might be the only decision that matters. For me, *it is*. If nothing else, I'm not afraid to meet God, and I'm not afraid of what happens when my time is up here. They say it's better to be safe than sorry. Interestingly, many people don't apply that concept to eternity.

An unbeliever has more to lose than a believer, and here is why. At the end of life, if they're wrong about God—if God is real and if everything the Bible said was true—they made a conscious decision to deny God and receive an eternity of turmoil and darkness.

But the believer—if they are wrong—they haven't lost anything. Obeying God only means loving God, yourself, and others. You receive what you put out into the world. Following God's instructions keeps us from self-destructive and self-sabotaging behaviors. Following God's commands causes us to be wise and it opens the door to more blessings. It leads us into a purposeful and meaningful existence, which is the root of fulfillment. So you win in life and you can't lose in the afterlife. It's a win-win scenario.

So, while we are asking the most important question in existence, what is honestly the best, wise, and sensible choice? One is win-win (believer), and one is lose-lose or win-lose at best (unbeliever). The *win* in their win-lose scenario is only possible if they are *actually* living a truly happy and fulfilling life on Earth.

Sin is self-destructive, so doing the opposite of what God advises isn't beneficial to your life any way you swing it. Believing in Jesus gives you standards, morals, and a purpose. It keeps you from living a miserable, meaningless, lost, dark, and confused life. There is no loss in believing.

Unbelievers are free to do whatever they choose without a conscience, but from experience, we know that is a dark, cold, empty, and unrewarding existence. Therefore, choosing to not believe only leads to the typical dysfunctional life, plus the added possibility of living the rest of eternity the same way you chose to live your life on earth—in misery.

Some people say we are in hell right now. Some believe in reincarnation. If that's true, let's just say…what if? If this is true, what if we keep coming back to this world over and over again after we die, *until* we learn and make the decision that Jesus is the way? Maybe some will eventually come around. Maybe some won't. So, what if we keep coming back to this place that is hell, but each time we come back, life gets better or worse depending on what we chose to believe in our past life? This is not my belief; however, I am saying, *what if?* My belief is in God's Word as it is.

But for those who believe otherwise, what if unbelieving means life gets harder and harder, darker and darker, less and less bearable, each time you return to earth (a.k.a. hell)? But, if this is the case, would you choose to keep coming back here over and over and over again with the world getting darker and darker as time goes on? Having no clue of how hard, dark, or sorrowful your next life would be. Having no clue which demons you will have to battle. You would be surrounded by people who think evil thoughts and choose an existence where love isn't important and doesn't matter?

Or would you rather leave this dark world behind? Would you rather get it 'right' right now, and go to a place known as heaven? A place where there is no more sickness and pain. A place where you are surrounded by people like you; people who believe in God's Word, love, and kindness. A place where there are no people who think it's okay to lie and kill and cheat.

Who deserves to go to this perfect and wonderful place? People who allowed God to change them? People who chose it? Again, imagine for a moment if everyone in the world obeyed Jesus and were loving and kind and forgiving and helpful towards one another. Maybe, just maybe, there is a place for people who have chosen to believe such a place exists. And when we go there, we don't have to worry about anyone coming in who doesn't believe in God's Word, love, and kindness. A place where there is no evil, no sickness, no aging.

And if you receive what you believe then...

End-of-Chapter Reflection

Chapter 5
To Believe or Not to Believe

1. Name three or more good reasons to believe in God. It can be anything you think of.

_____

_____

_____

_____

_____

_____

2. Name three or more sensible reasons NOT to believe in God (if applicable). What lasting or fulfilling benefits come with the reasons you listed?

_____

_____

_____

_____

3. What are your biggest takeaways from Chapter 5?

_____

_____

_____

_____

_____

_____

_____

4. How will you incorporate what you learned from Chapter 5 into your life today (and moving forward)?

_____

_____

_____

_____

_____

_____

_____

_____

5. Name something new that you discovered about yourself (if applicable).

_____

_____

_____

_____

_____

_____

_____

_____

_____

_____

6. Name something new or interesting that you learned about God, life, and/or people.

_____

_____

_____

_____

_____

_____

_____

7. Journal any other notes, takeaways, or reminders that you'd like to capture from Chapter 5.

_____

_____

_____

_____

_____

_____

_____

_____

_____

_____

_____

_____

Chapter 6

The Bible
a.k.a.
Answers

J ust about everything we operate comes with an instruction manual. It wouldn't make sense for an engineer to construct something complex for the world to use without offering instructions on how to use it. What creator would create a game and not provide rules on how to play it and how to win it?

I posed the following question and answer in Chapter 1: Why would our Creator create us, place us in this world, and not tell us how to live, win, lose, where to go, and what to do in this thing called life? The answer is He would not, and He did not.

We, as human beings, were not placed in this world with no compass or road map to give us the answers and direction we need in order to operate efficiently. The Bible is our instruction manual for life. It tells us everything we need to know in order to have everything we need in abundance, and no less.

The problem is, most people don't read the manual for themselves or simply refuse to believe and follow it. This is why the world is so dark and broken. Most go through life disregarding the instruction manual, which immediately and directly results in living in dysfunction and experiencing one problem after another.

"The whole Bible was given to us by inspiration from God and is useful to teach us what is TRUE and to make us realize what is wrong in our lives; It straightens us out and helps us do what is right. It is God's way of making us well prepared at every point, fully equipped to do good to everyone."
2 Timothy 3:16-17 TLB

The Bible is often referred to as:

Basic

Instructions

Before

Leaving

Earth

The Bible is how God speaks to us. It teaches us what He wants from us and how to live and thrive as human beings. The Bible is also known as The Word of God, God's Word, The Word, The Good News, and The Gospel.

The Bible is the most powerful, relevant, and essential book in existence. There is not one self-help book on the planet that contains any valuable and life-changing information that did not originate from a concept written in the Bible. All of the most powerful, influential, and transformational speakers in the world use techniques and advice derived from principles found in the Bible.

It's the highest-selling book of all time and has made a greater impact on the world than any other book ever written.

Some people say they don't believe in the Bible because man wrote it. I explain here, in general, and even deeper in Chapter 13 "Apologetics", why such a notion holds no merit.

God and His Word is the *only* thing in life that *does not* change. This is a definitive way to know that something is reliable and stable. Everything else in life changes constantly and sometimes in unexpected ways. But the most vital and important thing in life never changes. It does not waver. Jesus Christ is the same yesterday, today, and forever *(Hebrews 13:8)*. Therefore, the Bible has suitably been deemed, by many, to be the most reliable source of information on the planet.

So, how is it possible that something written *so* long ago has not required any content changes or updates over thousands of years? Simply put, because it is the *truth*. Because it is God. God and truth are constant, they are one and the same, and they don't change. That's what makes God and His Word reliable. It's the *only* thing in this world that doesn't change, hence our proof that there is only *one* truth. Even though the Bible was written thousands of years ago, its message is still relevant, impacting lives, and speaking truths about life today.

The Bible did not say one thing 800 years ago and something new today. This substantiates its truth, power, reliability, legitimacy, and validity. It is what it is: God's **unchanging** Word. Ergo, the truth can only be found in one place: The Bible. As you can see, the Bible is not only where God's Word and wisdom reside, it is where the *truth* resides. So when you need answers, the Bible is where you look.

Jesus proclaims in *John 14:6*, "I am the way, the *truth*, and the life."

"...*let God be true, but every man a liar.*"
Romans 3:4 NKJV

There was a time when it was widely taught and believed by society and healthcare specialists that "milk does a body good." Today, healthcare specialists say milk is not good for us. If you rely on and believe *solely* in human study, knowledge, and science, you are not building your life on a solid foundation. Human studies and science change on a regular basis. God's Word to us remains the same.

When you follow God and His Word, you have a solid foundation. When you follow any other source not derived from God's unchanging Word, you will not have stability in life. Everyone else says something one minute and another thing the next minute, because scientists and human beings discover new things as time goes on. There is nothing new to God. Therefore, who better to learn from than the Creator Himself?

Many people believe *only* in science, which changes like the wind. How strong is your foundation when what you choose to believe in is found to be invalid at any time and time after time? God is a million steps ahead of science. He created it. You are a million steps ahead as well, when you follow and look to God for guidance. We don't have to go through life lost and confused. That's what the Bible is for.

It's important to have the proper perspective when it comes to God, life, and truth. God's instructions are not restrictions, they are protection. Think about the problems you have experienced. Are those problems the direct result of doing the opposite of what God says?

When people argue against the Bible, it's because, as mentioned in Chapter 3, when it comes to our purpose in the world, we are at war. The adversary is successfully working through certain people to promote corruption everywhere we turn. I consider these to be the people who chose to be on a losing team because, no matter what it looks like, evil will never defeat good. The more people who turn away from God and His Word, the more evil and destruction we will see in the world. If you think about it, what loving parent wouldn't want their child to be good, loving, kind, and moral? Well, that's all the Bible and God ask of us.

How to Read the Bible

As mentioned in the previous chapter, people tend to focus on the wrong things when it comes to finding answers. That holds true when it comes to the Bible as well. Many people will ponder over whether certain things actually happened or if they're even possible, instead of focusing on the lesson and the powerful message the story is telling. The thing to understand is that there's much to be learned from Bible stories.

Every Bible story can be correlated to our experiences and they give us direction and guidance on how to view, approach, and overcome life's circumstances. No one can dispute that the Bible is packed with valuable, life-changing information, and more wisdom and great teachings than any other book that has ever been written. *That* is what we should be leveraging and focusing on. The rest is inconsequential.

Understanding the Bible

"I tried to read the Bible, but I don't understand it." Have you ever said or heard this statement? This is common, and there *is* a simple solution! The first key to understanding the Bible is figuring out which Bible version works for you and truly speaks to you.

The way people spoke in the olden days is quite different from the way we speak today. Fortunately, to help us understand God's Word better, there are several different translations—also known as versions—of the Bible. All of them pretty much say the same thing, just in different ways.

The reason for the different versions is due to the very question that started this section. Sometimes it's not what we say, but how we say it. The different translations give everyone the opportunity to really understand what the Bible is saying by communicating the same message in different ways. We all learn and interpret things differently. The Bible is such an important book, so great effort and attention is given towards ensuring it's not too complicated for us to understand.

Here is a side-by-side comparison of different versions of the same scripture. I took this screenshot from one of my favorite places to pull scripture: BibleHub.com. I usually Google the scripture, scroll until I see BibleHub, and then I click, and this displays...

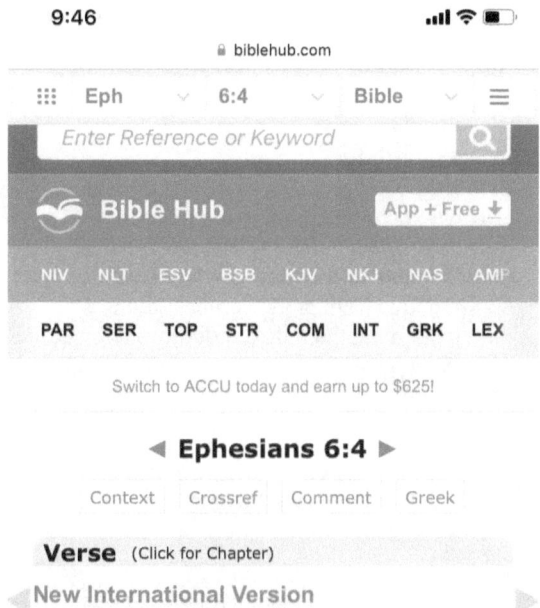

9:46

biblehub.com

Eph ∨ 6:4 ∨ Bible ∨ ≡

Enter Reference or Keyword

Bible Hub   App + Free ↓

NIV   NLT   ESV   BSB   KJV   NKJ   NAS   AMP

PAR   SER   TOP   STR   COM   INT   GRK   LEX

Switch to ACCU today and earn up to $625!

◀ **Ephesians 6:4** ▶

Context   Crossref   Comment   Greek

Verse (Click for Chapter)

New International Version
Fathers, do not exasperate your children; instead, bring them up in the training and instruction of the Lord.

New Living Translation
Fathers, do not provoke your children to anger by the way you treat them. Rather, bring them up with the discipline and instruction that comes from the Lord.

English Standard Version
Fathers, do not provoke your children to anger, but bring them up in the discipline and instruction of the Lord.

Berean Standard Bible
Fathers, do not provoke your children to wrath; instead, bring them up in the discipline and instruction of the Lord.

9:48

biblehub.com

⋮⋮⋮   Eph ⌄   6:4 ⌄   Bible ⌄ ☰

Amplified Bible
Fathers, do not provoke your children to anger [do not exasperate them to the point of resentment with demands that are trivial or unreasonable or humiliating or abusive; nor by showing favoritism or indifference to any of them], but bring them up [tenderly, with lovingkindness] in the discipline and instruction of the Lord.

Christian Standard Bible
Fathers, don't stir up anger in your children, but bring them up in the training and instruction of the Lord.

Holman Christian Standard Bible
Fathers, don't stir up anger in your children, but bring them up in the training and instruction of the Lord.

American Standard Version
And, ye fathers, provoke not your children to wrath: but nurture them in the chastening and admonition of the Lord.

Aramaic Bible in Plain English
Parents, do not anger your children, but rear them in the discipline and in the teaching of Our Lord.

Contemporary English Version
Parents, don't be hard on your children. Raise them properly. Teach them and instruct them about the Lord.

Douay-Rheims Bible

As you can see, they're all saying the same thing, just in different ways.

When you read one, you may like the way that version relays God's Word better than another. Or, if you don't understand the way one version is relaying a verse, you can refer to another version to help you understand it better. And what's cool is, you will understand it better simply because it was worded in a different way. One translation may not do anything for you, while another may resonate deeply and change your whole perspective! I love it! So, that's why you see different versions. Each version phrases the verses in its own way for the purpose of helping us understand God's Word better.

A few popular versions that you may have heard of include the King James Version (KJV), the New International Version (NIV), and the New Living Translation (NLT).

As you know, I personally love, read, and recommend a translation called The Living Bible (TLB), which was given to me by my Aunt Cora many years ago. I love TLB because it's translated into very easy-to-understand wording, which is similar to the verbiage we use today.

Another reason I *highly* recommend TLB is because you do NOT need a translator when you read this version. You don't need someone to decode the text or break it down for you. It's in a clear and simple form. If you have any questions, most will be the type that you can quickly and easily *Google*, because someone else has likely already asked that question.

For example, my son was reading TLB. He came and asked me why Jesus was called the Son of David. It's interesting because I didn't even know at the time. I hadn't read far enough in the

Old Testament. So, I simply Googled it—God is good—and there was the answer. It literally told me why and gave a reference. It told me where the answer was in the Bible, so I was able to read my Bible and test the information I was receiving!

If you're listening to a sermon and someone is reading from KJV or some version that you can't understand because of the phraseology, that means they have to tell you what it means. In my opinion, this is dangerous because many people have been led astray this way by false prophets or people who simply didn't know what they were talking about. Misinformation is a very real problem. When you're reading from a Bible that is simple enough for you to understand, you do NOT need a translator. You can learn directly from the Source. That's why I keep spreading the word about TLB. Today, with all of the misinformation and false prophecy going on, I thank God I have a Bible that I can read and learn from with little to no assistance.

Pick up a Bible translation that you understand so you won't have to rely on people to tell you what it says! Reading the same scripture in different translations usually helps you gain a better understanding of what the scripture is saying. Now you can sit quietly with God in your own home at any time, read your Bible, and know you are getting the right information—from the Source. Knowing the Bible for yourself, in this way, is what will help you be able to identify false prophets. If you don't know the Bible for yourself, you won't know when someone is telling you the wrong thing.

Another key. Before I read the Bible, every time, I say a rendition of this prayer:

Dear Heavenly Father,
Thank You for Your Word that I am about to receive.
Father, I ask that you eliminate any and all confusion and
misinterpretation. Please help me to receive Your
Word in the way that You intended.
In Jesus' Name I pray,
Amen.

I always feel warm and fuzzy after saying this prayer because I know God will deliver.

Once you've identified a Bible version that you like and is easy for you to understand, you can always compare it to other translations if you want. As we discussed, this will help you have a deeper understanding of the Word, and you'll be able to see the different ways that scripture is communicated.

When you type and search a particular scripture or keywords, it will pull up websites with Bible verses, which, on some sites like BibleHub, gives you several different translations with a side-by-side comparison. TLB isn't one of the most popular translations, so it may not pop up on the front screen of comparisons. But if you search for a verse followed by "TLB," it will show up. I absolutely love this side-by-side comparison feature. I usually have my TLB in hand and can compare it to the other translations that I see on BibleHub.

A version with words that resonate best within you and that you understand would be the Bible translation that I would suggest for you to read!

I personally don't understand some of the other versions as well myself. Because of their wording, they don't speak to me or reach me the same way The Living Bible does. I have found TLB to be extremely transformational for me. Once you realize which translation speaks to you, you will be very excited to keep reading. You'll get wiser and stronger with every word. The confusion in life will begin to clear as you receive truth and clarity from our Father, the Creator Himself. There's nothing more therapeutic because when you are listening to and learning from God, you are walking in light and purpose. This is where true fulfillment begins.

Another reason reading the Bible in its entirety is so important is because the more you read, the more things begin to connect and make sense. Many answers come as you continue reading, learning, and growing. Having a Bible that is easy to read doesn't mean you will understand *everything* it says, at least not right away.

Remember the keys you've learned. I've come across things in the Bible that I didn't completely understand, but they had nothing to do with clarifying life or providing direction. It was just *information* that I didn't understand. Here is the distinction: There is information that makes a world of difference, and then there is just *information*. It's not about understanding everything, it's about understanding what's important and what makes a difference. It's about focusing on what you know, not the things you don't know. The Bible tells us more than enough in order for us to find peace, clarity, direction, and fulfillment in our lives. Thankfully, these are the things of the Bible that *are* easy to understand.

1 Corinthians 13:12 makes it clear that we aren't meant to understand everything right now, but someday we will.

Where to Begin

You may be wondering where to begin reading the Bible. The Living Bible that I have is an older copy (over thirty years old), and it has a section at the beginning titled "Where to Begin," which I will share with you because this actually worked great for me. If you would like to receive a free copy of "Where to Begin" instructions and the step-by-step guide that I followed when I began reading the Bible, visit www.LatinaNicholeSmith.com/free for your free guide.

Also, while reading this book, definitely begin with reading all of the scripture references as you go along!

So…should you start in the Old Testament or the New Testament and what's the difference?

The Old Testament vs. The New Testament

The Old Testament is from the beginning of time, before Jesus lived on Earth. In the Old Testament, there was no sacrifice sufficient enough to cover our sins (the unrighteousness of man). Out of God's grace and love for us came the New Testament (covenant, law, or agreement), which began after Jesus was born. The new law states that we are saved by faith, believing that Jesus is the Son of God who was crucified by men, as a living sacrifice for our sins, and resurrected from the dead three days later by God. If we believe and accept Jesus as our Lord and Savior, we are saved. This is the basis of Christianity.

The law now, and forevermore, is that we are to love the Lord with all our heart, mind, and soul, and love each other as we love ourselves.

"Jesus replied, 'Love the Lord your God with all your heart, soul, and mind. This is the first and greatest commandment. The second most important is similar: 'Love your neighbor as much as you love yourself.' All other commandments and all the demands of the prophets stem from these two laws and are fulfilled if you obey them. Keep only these and you will find that you are obeying all the others.'"
Mathew 22:37-40 TLB

So again, it's all about love. Once we accept Jesus and simply ask for forgiveness of our sins, we are forgiven. Then, with the help of God's Holy Spirit, we begin to transform. The validity of our faith is demonstrated through love—love for God, love for self, and love for others. *This* is what faith is. The Ten Commandments is a great guide that teaches us what love looks like and how to love. We talk more about this in the next chapter!

So, where to begin? I recommend starting in the New Testament, as did the "Where to Begin" instructions which are free for you to download. The New Testament is easy to follow and understand, as long as you are reading a translation with verbiage that is simplified and direct, as discussed (TLB, NIV, NLT, and more).

When I began, I wanted to start in the New Testament because I wanted to know what God was expecting of me right now. We live under the new law, so that's where I wanted to start. I read the entire New Testament, then I went to the beginning of the Old Testament (Genesis) where it all began, and I read in order from there. I did not read the New Testament in order. I followed the instructions we talked about, which again, are free for you to download. It explains which books to read first and why!

I'm going to get technical just for a moment. For anyone who might not be familiar, a "book" of the Bible is Mark, Acts, Romans, James, Genesis, and so on. Within the books are chapters, identified by a large number, which starts every chapter. Within each chapter are verses, identified by a tiny number, which starts every verse. Example: Romans 6:16 (Book, chapter: verse).

In the Old Testament, there are a couple of sections (parts of Leviticus and Numbers) which may not be as easy to follow because they're not all stories. Much of these sections specifically describe the laws God gave for His people to follow in the Old Testament including several building specifications and other technicalities. Besides this, as long as you are reading from an easy-to-understand translation, you should have no trouble following along and enjoying the many amazing stories you'll read. They're not only insightful and interesting, but they are packed with great examples, encouragement, wisdom, and guidance!

The New Testament, on the other hand, will teach you all about who Jesus really is. If you pay attention to Jesus' character and what He values and asks of us, you will see why He is worth following and trusting. You'll begin to really know and love Him.

Once you have read the New Testament, you can then go back to Genesis to see how it all began. There are many great stories in the Old Testament and throughout the Bible. Many of these stories depict situations that we face today and provide encouragement and direction for us.

Knowing God and the Bible for yourself is paramount so that you won't succumb to being taught the wrong information. Remember this scripture:

"Dear friends, do not believe everyone who claims to speak by the spirit. You must test them to see if the spirit they have comes from God. For there are many false prophets in the world."
1 John 4:1 NLT

Matthew 7:15-20 tells you **in detail** what to look out for and how to identify a good spirit, so make sure you read it and reread it from time to time. This will help strengthen your discernment. The following scripture describes the characteristics of God's Spirit, The Holy Spirit.

"But when the Holy Spirit controls our lives He will produce this kind of fruit in us: love, joy, peace, patience, kindness, goodness, faithfulness, gentleness, and self-control...
Those who belong to Christ Jesus have nailed the passions and desires of their sinful nature to His cross and crucified them there."
Galatians 5:22-24 TLB

Remember, having your own personal relationship with God is what's important. You should read and know what the Bible says for yourself. Be sure not to learn small pieces here and there. Know the entire context surrounding the scripture to be sure of exactly what it's saying or referring to so that it cannot be taken out of context or misinterpreted.

People often take scripture out of context and misinterpret it. Cherry-picking Bible verses can be catastrophic, and in doing so, people often fail to understand what God is really saying. For example, in the book of Ecclesiastes, King Solomon is giving his *opinion* and explaining how *he* sees and feels about the world. But the last two verses in the book of Ecclesiastes give his conclusion about God and life. These last two verses (found in *Ecclesiastes 12:13-14*) are conclusive, but people will miss this if they've only read Chapter 9 of that book.

This is just an example of how vital it is to read and know an *entire* book, not just bits and pieces. There's often a conclusion, within or at the end of a book, which makes the stance of the passage clear. It's important to have a *complete* picture of what God is saying.

I wouldn't be too concerned about how long it will take to read the entire Bible. If you get into the habit of reading it every day and going book-by-book, you'll eventually have read it all. It's more about spending time with God daily, learning more and more about Him, growing in faith and wisdom, and developing a personal relationship with Him.

The first thing I do every morning is talk to God in prayer and then read the Bible. I don't have a set amount that I read; I just make sure I read it every day. If I read a paragraph, I'm happy and I've accomplished my goal that day. If I read a whole page or more, even better. But my minimum goal is simply to read it every day, initially starting at the beginning of a book and reading that entire book from start to finish.

Now that we know more about the Bible and where the answers are, let's move on and talk about "The Special Sauce" that brings it all together!

End-of-Chapter Reflection

Chapter 6
Bible a.k.a Answers

1. What is the most reliable source of information on the planet, and what makes it reliable?

_____

_____

_____

_____

_____

_____

2. What are your biggest takeaways from Chapter 6?

_____

_____

_____

_____

_____

_____

3. How will you incorporate what you learned from Chapter 6 into your life today (and moving forward)?

_____

_____

_____

_____

_____

_____

_____

4. Name something new that you discovered about yourself (if applicable).

_____

_____

_____

_____

_____

_____

5. Name something new or interesting that you learned about the Bible, God, life, and/or people.

_____

_____

_____

_____

_____

_____

_____

_____

_____

6. Journal any other notes, takeaways, or reminders that you'd like to capture from Chapter 6.

_____

_____

_____

_____

_____

_____

Chapter 7

Obedience: "The Special Sauce"

There are some who believe that sin, the Bible, God, and His commandments are things constructed just to keep us all under control. But, if we are honest, we need a degree of control and order as human beings for the simple fact that everyone doesn't always choose to do what is just, right, fair, or kind.

Now that we know the key to escaping a life of dysfunction is following our Creator's remedy for success, and now that we know where all of the answers are, I'd like to discuss obedience a little deeper. Obedience is "The Special Sauce." Obedience is the ingredient that activates the promises, power, and favor of God in our lives. This component is extremely important, yet difficult for most.

There are a few reasons obeying God isn't easy for most. One reason is because most individuals do not like being told what to do. Many humans have a rebellious nature, whether consciously or unconsciously. You'll find out why in the next chapter.

The world has widely adopted the perception that we need to be free to do whatever we want. Most people think we are fools to let any authority restrict us from doing the things we want to do.

Authority is a great thing when it is rooted in love, protection, and respect for others. This type of authority is necessary in order for us to thrive because of the many evil influences that are ever-present in this world. The right authority, who lives by good morals and pure principles and who encourages us to do things that are good for ourselves and others, is a beautiful thing. That is exactly what the Word of God does for us.

God encourages us to stay away from sin. But what is sin?

> *"Everyone who sins is breaking God's law, for*
> *all <u>sin is contrary to the law of God</u>."*
> *1 John 3:4 NLT*

Other Bible translations define sin as lawlessness. To put it simply, sin is anything opposite of what God commands. My simplified definition of sin is anything that is destructive or harmful to yourself or others; because anything destructive or harmful to yourself or others is not love for others nor love for self, which is God's ultimate commandment—*love*. Since God created us, He knows exactly what type of behaviors we need to refrain from in order to operate at our highest level as human beings. Considering we don't have the infinite wisdom God has, we can't always see how certain actions can bring harm to us and our lives until it's too late.

It's no different from any other type of creator. Let's take electronics, for example. The creator can tell us exactly what to do and what not to do in order for that product to function properly. If it malfunctions, they can tell us how to remedy it.

Having the proper perspective when it comes to obedience makes all the difference in the world.

"For, dear brothers, you have been given freedom:
not freedom to do wrong, but freedom to love each other."
Galatians 5:13 TLB

A great way to look at this scripture and obedience is this: we don't *have* to love, we *get* to love. We don't *have* to do good, we *get* to do good.

God gives us an illustration to help us understand how we have *two* choices that affect our entire life for better or for worse, and we choose one or the other every day. We can choose to be a slave to something that is destroying us, or we can choose to be a slave to something that flourishes us. *Romans 6:16-23* is a must-read! It explains this concept of how we are either a slave to the flesh (human behaviors) or the Spirit (the ways of God). When you are a slave to something, like the flesh, that means it controls you. This is the case for most people, which is why life sucks for most. This is not freedom as many misconceive it to be.

If something controls you and you obey it, it is your master, and you are a slave to it. For example, many people lack self-control. When we do things that we know aren't good for us, it's either because we lack wisdom, don't love ourselves, or we can't help it—meaning we can't control ourselves. Any of these are possible but it's usually because we can't control ourselves. In this case, our flesh controls us, making us a slave to the flesh. If it wants something and it tells you to do it, you do it, even when you know it's hurting you.

On the contrary, when we are controlled by God, we are in good hands because *everything* God commands and leads us to do is incredibly good for us and it benefits everyone around us. The devil doesn't love anyone, not even himself. He wants you to be like him. This is why he continually sends temptations your way—to keep you trapped and bound in misery. And he wants you to believe there's nothing you can do about it, but the devil is a liar. Understanding this key will change your life. I say again, we have *two* choices that affect our entire life for better or for worse, and we choose one or the other every day.

Lastly, with this in mind, and with the lack of self-control and decision-making skills that are evident in everyday human behavior, would you rather be controlled by the infinitely good and wise Spirit of God or controlled by you in the flesh? For a deeper understanding, again, be sure to read *Romans 6:16-23*. Within this scripture, the Bible poses an interesting question—you've been living in sin and disobedience thus far, how has that worked out for you?

To be clear, disobedience leads to a dysfunctional life of sin, which is a never-ending quest for happiness and fulfillment. You may already know this from experience. Nothing about habitual sin leads to happiness, but rather, the opposite. Why we do the things we do and how to master this, is something we learn in the next chapter!

Remember, God does not give us commandments so life will suck. God gives us commandments so life *won't* suck! Once you are able to shift your mentality and look at life from the right per-spective—God's perspective—your life *will* change for the better.

If you know what God advises, it's wise to obey because great reward and success will always come from it. Obeying God is the planting of good seeds, which bring a sweet harvest and give us so much to live for and look forward to. Obedience is not something we should be resentful about. We should be happy to obey God! We should be happy that we have a Creator and Heavenly Father who loves us and who has given us direction, answers, and guide-lines that lay a direct path to prosperity. Most look at God's commandments as a downer, which is a childlike perspective and a reason many operate in dysfunction on a regular basis.

In the last chapter, we learned from Jesus Himself *(Matthew 22:37-40 TLB)* that we will find ourselves in compliance with all laws when we keep these two: (1) love the Lord with all our hearts, mind, and soul…and (2) love others as we love ourselves. Love. But in order to do that, we *must* know what love is and we must know how to love. What is love?

"Love is patient, love is kind. It does not envy, it does not boast, it is not proud. It does not dishonor others, it is not self-seeking, it is not easily angered, it keeps no record of wrongs. Love does not delight in evil but rejoices with the truth. It always protects, always believes, always hopes, always perseveres. Love never fails…"
1 Corinthians 13:4-8

This scripture tells us *what* love is. God's commandments tell us *how*. Following God's commandments is a display of love. Love for God, love for self, and love for others. One key factor that *most* miss is that obedience to God *is* self-love. God's commandments are a guide which helps us live in peace and harmony with ourselves, as well as one another. I mentioned in another chapter that the Ten Commandments is a great life guide to follow, as a basis, because the Ten Commandments teach us how to love *and respect* ourselves, God, and others. Following the Ten Commandments, as a basis, results in a flowing river of greatness and good favor.

Obeying God's Ten Commandments helps you establish who you are and helps you develop a strong, solid sense of self. When you have these types of values, you become someone *you* can love and respect, and others will too. It leads to self-love and so many more wonderful benefits. Self-love reduces self-destructive behavior as opposed to sin. It's a sweeter life. So, definitely start there! Everything takes practice, and when you do it long enough, it becomes natural! It becomes *who you are*. Something so amazing all starts with simply trusting, listening to, and following the Lord.

The Ten Commandments

1. *"I am the LORD your God. You shall have no other gods before me."*
2. *"You shall not make for yourselves any idol—or any likeness of what is in heaven above, or on the earth beneath, or in the water under the earth—as an object to worship, serve, or bow down to."*
3. *"You shall not misuse nor take the name of the LORD your God in vain."*
4. *"Remember to observe the Sabbath day by keeping it holy."*

5. *"Honor your father and your mother."*
6. *"You shall not kill."*
7. *"You shall not commit adultery."*
8. *"You shall not steal."*
9. *"You shall not lie by giving falsehoods against, or to, your neighbor [any person]."*
10. *"You shall not covet [that is: to selfishly desire, lust over, and attempt to acquire] your neighbor's house, wife, or anything that belongs to your neighbor [any person]."*
Exodus 20:2-17

Considering that the greatest amount of pain we face is at the hand and actions of other human beings, how much less pain would we suffer if more people did as God commands us? Don't kill, don't steal, don't cheat, be humble, be kind, be honest, forgive, love, help, give, give, give. These are a few examples of what love looks like, and they are evidence of a good and honorable God. People will tell their kids that Santa is real but not God who only encourages us to love ourselves and others. Funny world isn't it?

Yes, life can be hard for reasons we don't always understand right away. However, how much easier would it be if we had loving and kind people around us through those hard times? Furthermore, what type of world would this be if we didn't have God's loving commandments as a guide and motivating factor?

You can probably admit that anytime you have ignored God's instruction, it didn't turn out well. It may have felt good in the moment or temporarily, but in the end, it likely only made matters worse, leaving you empty and bitter inside.

The truth is, having decent core values and a moral guide helps keep you from making poor and self-destructive decisions.

So you see, God's commandments are not designed to control us but to set us free from the entrapment and the destructive nature of sin. God's commandments are for our protection and offer us direction. Once you're able to wrap your mind around these concepts, you can see how having commandments from God is a good thing, not a bad thing. Before now, you may not have liked the idea of the word *command*. But now, I hope you can see the love, honor, and the necessity in our heavenly Father's way.

We give commandments, or rules, to our children out of love and to protect them. "*Stay away from that crowd, don't touch that, no more candy, eat your vegetables,*" and so on. As good parents, we give our children orders because we love them and we know what's best for them, not to control them.

What has happened with the vast majority of the world is they have adopted a child's mentality when it comes to getting and doing what they want. A child doesn't like to be told what to do, even by someone who has a higher intelligence or experience level than them and who is only trying to love and protect them. *This* is the same mentality of those who find it hard to obey God or other appropriate and decent authority figures and guidelines.

It's easy to know when an authority figure is good because they make commandments that are beneficial for everyone. They don't make commands that only benefit themselves or a select group of individuals.

Stop for a moment and think about why certain rules, laws, and God's commandments are in place. They keep you safe, lead to a better future, offer better outcomes, and improve your quality of life. Can you see how following them will lead you down the best and most prosperous path? Childlike minds can't grasp this concept.

> *"When I was a child, I spoke as a child,*
> *I understood as a child, I thought as a child;*
> *but when I became a man, I put away childish things."*
> *1 Corinthians 13:11 NKJV*

As there is a necessity in life to have rules and guidelines to keep the world a safer and less chaotic place, there is a necessity for God to give us guidance and standards. Every one of them benefits us. Having this correct mentality, mindset, and perspective will make God's commandments far easier to understand and obey. The wise understand that obedience to God releases us from the grip of this dysfunctional, lost, and dark world. *This* is true freedom.

5 Steps Forward, 10 Steps Back

Besides the fact that sin separates us from God, there is always a detrimental price associated with sin, which is why God advises us to turn away from it. This is also why turning away from sin is self-love. One area that many may struggle to abandon, and may feel is the hardest and ultimate sacrifice, is refraining from sex outside of marriage. This is probably the one that makes many hesitant to go all in, as premarital sex is highly normalized in society, especially today. But I want to give a few examples of how engaging in any sin is always self-destructive and never worth the price. It will always bring a 5 steps forward, 10 steps back type of result in life.

Fornication (and any other sex sin) is mentioned throughout the Bible as something that God advises against. Fornication is the act of having sex outside of marriage. Now, I know, I know! This is the area that gets the most people. Hey, I used to be one of them! The idea of no sex until marriage is as ancient as dinosaurs! I get it, but when it comes to obedience to God and how this protects us, let's break this down. If you happen to be someone who is hesitant to commit your life to God and His way because of this, let's discuss how God's commandment of refraining from premarital sex actually leads to a better life.

Premarital sex provides temporary satisfaction. It is some-thing you must do over and over. The pleasure is gone soon after it ends. It's like a drug. It can lead to sexual addictions, sexually transmitted diseases, heartbreak, and toxic soul ties to many peo-ple (often the wrong people). It can lead to unintended pregnancies and a whole slew of other issues. The worldly choice is to partake freely in premarital sex, but it's much wiser to listen to God who loves you, wants the best for you, and is trying to protect you from actions that will only cause you problems and less happiness down the road.

Now, I'm not saying whether or not someone is going to burn in hell for these things! That's not my call. I'm just saying that if God doesn't approve of certain behaviors, you might not *really* want to find out why.

My point is this—life can be hard, but it doesn't always have to be. We can take the smooth road or the bumpy road. But God, our Provider, absolutely tells us everything we need to know. We just need to read and *actually* apply it. We just have to care more about what God says and wants than what we or anyone else says and wants. That's when we begin to experience exceedingly and abundantly more than we could ever ask or imagine *(Ephesians 3:20).*

Lying is a common behavior that is hard for some to break. I've heard the statement far too many times that "everybody lies." Many people have normalized lying and underestimated the demise associated with lying. One thing that few understand is that anything you get the wrong way will *not* last. For some reason, many fail to realize that getting anything the wrong way is NEVER worth it in the end and is a complete waste of time and effort *(Jeremiah 17:11).*

Getting things the wrong way in life is like building a house or empire on sinking sand. Why do the wrong things and put years of time and effort into a relationship, business, or whatever it may be just for it all to come crashing down one day? That's exactly what happens when we try to get ahead by lying, cheating, stealing, or any other unrighteous act which God warns us against *(Matthew 7:24-27).*

When we do and get things the right way, we don't have to worry about it crashing down later. We don't have to worry about losing it. We won't have to work so hard to keep it or be filled with anxiety and fear of losing it. That can all be eliminated by just doing the right thing. We know what to do because the Creator tells us in His Word and it's evident in everyday life how unruly behaviors only destroy our own lives and those around us.

If we are walking in righteousness and we get something the right way yet we still lose it, it's part of God's plan. Expect an upgrade.

Engaging in sin, again, brings a 5 steps forward and 10 steps back type of life. No one will ever get ahead by continuously doing the wrong thing. On the outside, sometimes it looks as though evil acts and evil men are prosperous. That's an illusion.

> *"Be still in the presence of the LORD, and wait patiently*
> *for Him to act. Don't worry about evil people who prosper*
> *or fret about their wicked schemes."*
> *Psalms 37:7 NLT*

Evil people are usually suffering greatly in ways you don't see and they will eventually lose it all or will lose the things they love and want the most. The price of sin and disobedience is costly, and it's never worth it. Understanding this core concept is the key to escaping a life of setbacks, dysfunction, and defeat.

Following God's commands is easier said than done for most, so how? How can I make this transition and change my ways for a better life and a better future? Great questions!

I will be providing the answers in the next chapter. We're going to learn more about ourselves and our nature as human beings. We're going to discuss why we do the things we do and what it takes to counter our natural self-destructive tendencies. Once we know and understand why we do the things we do, we are less likely to succumb to the subconscious thoughts, feelings, and behaviors that regularly lead to our own demise! There is a solution!

End-of-Chapter Reflection

Chapter 7
Obedience: "The Special Sauce"

1. What key factor (on our part) changes everything and unlocks the door to a better you, a better life, and a better world? (one word)

_____

2. What are your biggest takeaways from Chapter 7?

_____

_____

_____

_____

_____

_____

_____

_____

_____

3. How will you incorporate what you learned from Chapter 7 into your life today (and moving forward)?

_____

_____

_____

_____

_____

_____

_____

_____

4. Name something new that you discovered about yourself (if applicable).

_____

_____

_____

_____

_____

_____

_____

5. Name something new or interesting that you learned about God, life, and/or people.

_____

_____

_____

_____

_____

_____

6. Journal any other notes, takeaways, or reminders that you'd like to capture from Chapter 7.

_____

_____

_____

_____

_____

_____

_____

Chapter 8

Why We Do the Things We Do

Have you ever found yourself asking, "Why did I do that?" or "What is wrong with me?" Have you ever felt like you don't understand yourself at all? Have you ever wondered, "What is wrong with people?" or "Why is the world the way it is?"

This chapter is designed to answer these very questions. As you know, my "go-to" and belief is that the answers to all of our questions are in the Bible.

I'll be sharing a few scriptures with you which will help you have a better understanding of the world and mankind. This is another chapter that I'm very excited about because it gives insight into a very important aspect of us, as humans. Being aware of our natural make-up and our natural tendencies as humans make it much easier to circumnavigate some of the dumb things we tend to do regularly, without even knowing or understanding why we do them.

As human beings, we're naturally drawn to things that are not good for us. Shocking right? The foods we love the most are the worst for us. The relationship partners we tend to gravitate toward often leave us wondering, in retrospect, *what in the world was I thinking?*

We've discussed the fact that sin is self-destructive and that obedience, or in other words, actually listening to what God says, is the key to escaping dysfunction. If we know that wisdom comes from God and obedience will lead us down a road of happiness and fulfillment, why is it so hard to do? I'm glad you asked!

In the first section of this chapter, we are going to talk about the world, the people in it, and what's really going on. In the second half, we are going to discuss why we struggle to do the things we should and how to overcome this.

I'd like to start by sharing some important factors about the world we live in according to the Bible. *Hebrews 13:14* tells us that this world is *not* our home. The world we live in, and now know, is a temporary place. *2 Corinthians 4:4* tells us that the devil is the ruler of *this* world. Correspondingly, *this* is the devil's stomping ground. That's why you see so much evil and darkness in the world and in so many people. Jesus speaks to this in *John 8:44 NIV:*

"You belong to your father, the devil, and you want to carry out your father's desires. He was a murderer from the beginning, not holding to the truth, for there is no truth in him. When he lies, he speaks his native language, for he is a liar and the father of lies."

Jesus is telling us here that when someone acts like the devil, that proves he (the devil) is their father. He's the one they are influenced by, and they are a contributor to the darkness of this world, like their father. Jesus tells us in *John 10:10* that the thief comes only to steal, kill, and destroy.

The devil has children, and they act like him. They delight in the same things the devil delights in, and they too come to steal, kill, and destroy. Sometimes they do this to people literally, and sometimes figuratively. They can steal your belongings or they can steal your faith, your joy, your self-esteem, and your sanity if you aren't vigilant. Jesus tells us in *Matthew 7:15-20* that you know a tree by the fruit it bears. That means you can identify people by their actions. In this scripture, Jesus affirms that a good tree *does not* bear bad fruit.

Once a person has shown you who they are, believe them. Once you see what kind of fruit they bear, you know exactly who they belong to and who sent them. Don't overlook red flags. These are not the type of people you should allow close enough to harm or influence you. Don't hate them, pray for them, but definitely keep a safe distance. That is, if you don't want to open yourself up to being misled, negatively influenced, or hurt by such people.

This is the very reason we need to always evaluate people by how they act, not only by what they say. The same applies to people who claim to be Christians or sent by God. We talk more about this in the next chapter and in Chapter 12.

If a person claims they love you, the truth is in their character, their behavior, and the things they do. Remember, God gives us the description and definition of love in *1 Corinthians 13*.

The Bible reminds us to put our trust only in God, not in man *(Psalms 118:8)*, because not only is the devil a liar, but he is a good one. He is deceptive, charming, influential, and persuasive. Having a close relationship with God and being filled with God's

Holy Spirit gives us a keen radar against these types. It's called discernment. Another reason it's always best to walk closely with God in this world.

Whether we know it or not, our actions, one way or another, have a direct impact on the world and either strengthen the devil's cause or God's cause. How so?

Kindness is contagious but so is unkindness. I say this because as humans, if someone loves us, we tend to love them back, and vice versa. If someone dislikes or mistreats us, we tend to dislike them as well. If people won't let us move over in traffic, we might be less likely to let others move over in traffic, and so on. This is why I say kindness is contagious, as well as unkindness.

In Chapter 3 we talked about the war between good and evil. But why is it that the forces of darkness and evil are more prominent than the forces of good? One reason is that, as mentioned, this is the devil's world, his playground. He has many children here who are influencing the minds and behaviors of others.

In the story of the two brothers, we discussed how the dysfunction in society is largely related to the fact that human beings often copy the behavior of other human beings, even when that behavior is obviously dark, self-destructive, and has no benefits.

Few recognize the importance of doing the right and wise thing regardless of what others do. Few acknowledge the fact that human beings do what *they* want to do, not what God wants them to do. The elect don't blame God for the actions of human beings. Yes, God made us, *but* He gave us the freedom to make our own decisions. He didn't make puppets. Any human being can decide to listen to God and be kind. We all have a common knowledge of the difference between right and wrong. Personally, if I was going to create people and give them a choice between the two, I would think they would all be insightful enough to choose the right thing as well.

This brings us back to Chapter 1, "Why Life Sucks." If you drive a car into the ocean, it will sink. It will malfunction because it's operating outside of what it was purposed and created to do. Now, according to Albert Einstein, the definition of insanity is "doing the same thing over and over and expecting a different result." If what you have been doing isn't working...if emulating everything you see others doing in this broken world isn't working...it's time to realize that maybe they are all doing it wrong. Maybe being different from the world is the way to go. God advises us to do just that in *Romans 12:2 NIV* which states, "*Do not conform to the pattern of this world, but be transformed by the renewing of your mind.*"

When God made us, He gave us free will. He created us, giving us the freedom to decide what we will do and how we will act. At *any* moment we can change our own lives by paying attention to what controls us and making conscious decisions on what we allow to be influencing factors in our lives.

Some people are an example of what to do, and some people are an example of what *not* to do. Which ones will you follow? Which ones do you follow? What do you allow to influence and direct your life, your thoughts, and your actions? Do your habits lead you toward becoming the person you want to be and acquiring the things you want to acquire, or do they take you farther away?

Having a good life does require *thinking*. It requires paying attention to what is going on around you and evaluating whether it is helping or hindering you. Then, you have to be willing to cease engagement with anything that is proven destructive in your life. That is when the smoke begins to clear. *That* is how you clear out darkness and begin to see the light of day.

The Spirit vs. the Flesh

So, now that we have a better understanding of the world we live in, let's talk about ourselves as human beings. Why do we do the things we do? Why is it so much easier to do the wrong thing than the right thing? Why do we crave and navigate toward the very things we shouldn't? Great questions. Here's why.

Just as there are two opposing forces at war in the world—good and evil, there are two opposing forces within us as human beings which are at war—the flesh and the Spirit. *Galatians 5:16-25* explains, in detail, about these two opposing forces and tells us exactly how to identify when we are a person who is controlled by the flesh and how to identify when we are one who is controlled by the Spirit. We will view these scriptures towards the end of this chapter. *Galatians 5:16-25* also tells us how we can curve our strong, natural, fleshly desires and become one who obeys the Spirit more easily, more readily, and more naturally. Reading that scripture will give you a thorough understanding of the information we are about to discuss and will really help you understand yourself better as a human being! I enjoy the TLB version because it's very well said and easy to understand.

The flesh is controlled by our earthly bodies and worldly desires. We were born into sin, so our flesh is easily influenced by this world and the things of this world. When you're living in the Spirit, the Spirit of God is in control of you and your life. Even though we were born with a sinful nature, the flesh is *not* stronger than the Spirit, just as evil is *not* stronger than good. So we have God (the Spirit, goodness, love) who is opposed to the devil (the flesh, evil, sin).

Again, the flesh is *not* more powerful than the Spirit. God, the Spirit, goodness, and love are the highest powers. Evil, the flesh, sin, and the devil have *no* power unless you give it to them *(Luke 10:19)*. Remember, God gave us free will, so God doesn't make you choose Him. *You* decide which influences you will succumb to and be controlled by. It is a choice, 100 percent.

How to Overcome the Flesh

So, here it is, the answer we've been waiting for! How do we overcome our natural tendency to sin?

Before I provide the answer, it's foundational for me to give a little backstory.

In *Genesis 6:5-7*, we learned God was sorry He made man, because their evil tendencies filled the earth. God made a decision to wipe all evil from the earth with a great flood (Noah's story), but when the world repopulated again, so did more and more evil people.

If you've ever read the Old Testament, you know that God tried and tried to rid evil from the earth, but man has free will, and people have consistently *chosen* to disregard God's instruction and live sinful lives *(2 Kings 17:13-20).* It's like nothing God said or did made a difference. Kind of like today. Who actually listens to God?

Nowadays, many people want to take God out of everything because the false prophets, that God warns us about, make godliness look bad. They are phonies. They pretend to be godly or sent by God, when they are not *(Matthew 7:15-23).* Their fruit and their actions show who they really are and who they belong to. These individuals prove they aren't of God, yet no one listens to God in reference to this, they just turn against Him. As you can see, the devil's tricks work on many.

At the time of this writing, school mass shootings were at an all-time high. Let me remind you that for years, many people have been petitioning to take any mention of God out of schools. So, God has been kicked out of schools and we wonder why they don't seem like a safe place anymore. People keep trying to remove God from the world, so in essence, God gives them a world without Him. Again, He will let us have our own way. He will not force Himself upon us.

People petition for God to be removed then ask where He is and why isn't He doing anything. People have serious double standards. They want God to do everything they say but don't want to do what God says. They want to kick Him out and then blame Him for something He wasn't involved in.

Throughout the Old Testament, there are several occasions where God wiped out thousands and thousands of people. God did this to *remove* evil. It's interesting to me that people will ask,

"Why does God allow evil to go on?" But they ridicule and question His character for wiping out evil in the Old Testament. Okay. So, now He doesn't do that anymore.

God saw that it doesn't matter what He does or how many evil people He wipes out; they're like roaches: They don't die, they multiply!

God decided He would do something different. This is where the New Testament begins, as we learned in Chapter 6. God decided that He would allow a part of Himself, His son Jesus, to come to Earth, not only to save us from sin and death, but to put Himself in our shoes and know, first hand, what it's like to live in this dark world as a child of God.

Jesus and God are one *(John 10:30)*. Therefore, Jesus has the *power* of God and God's Holy Spirit within Him. We will never be perfect, as Jesus is; however, the same gift that Jesus has, God's Holy Spirit, is the same gift and power that God extends to us when we decide to accept this priceless gift.

Jesus sacrificed His life to cover the sins of man and wipe their slate clean with God. Man's solution is to accept this offering and sacrifice.

Man now has the *choice* to accept the gift of being saved and freed from their evil human nature and the grip of sin. If man chooses to have faith in Jesus, the Savior of man, they can inherit the Spirit of God, which leads us into righteousness and salvation. It's not something we work for. This is what it means to be saved by faith alone and not by works. Anyone can accept this free gift of salvation, at any time, by choice. We aren't saved because of anything we did but because of what Jesus did. We accept Jesus as our Lord and Savior, who then gives us a Helper, the Holy Spirit, who comes in and cleanses us. One's faith isn't saving or even real if it doesn't change you. We talk about this in Chapter 11.

Man can now welcome and invite the Spirit of God to come and live within him and to guide and control his every step and his every thought. Your fleshly nature and desires are nailed to the cross, and they die there. You become a new creature, or born again, with a new Spirit who overpowers the flesh. So it's not *us* who have the power to do right. It's the power of God working within us through His Holy Spirit.

When you make the decision to give your life to Christ, you don't have to battle the flesh with your own might. It's the Spirit and power of God who leads us to have the desire and ability to live a life of obedience. *Only* the Spirit of God has total power over the flesh. If you've been trying to do it on your own, that's why it hasn't been working. We *need* God. He is the source that we *must* be connected to in order to live and flourish as we were created to.

Be sure to take the time to read *Romans Chapters 6-8*. These scriptures just about sum up the dysfunction of man and provide an understanding of human nature and a perspective so effective that it can absolutely lead to a shift in our behavior and choices. It explains in clear detail what we just discussed here. Many allow their lives to be controlled by the flesh, which is cataclysmic. The flesh naturally navigates toward sin which is always self-destructive, as we know. The Holy Spirit is the opposite of that and the key to escaping a life of dysfunction, confusion, darkness, and defeat.

So we now have our answer. How do we live a good life free from sin and poor decision-making? It's by giving Jesus permission to come into your heart and take over. It's by asking Jesus to come in and take control or "take the wheel," as some say. It's by surrendering and succumbing to the will of God. Because He will *not* force Himself on us.

Next Steps

Now, what is it that helps us be successful after we've accepted Jesus? Reading the Bible daily, regularly, and meditating on what it says *(2 Peter 1:2-11 'TLB version recommended'),* and by talking to God regularly (praying). This helps us grow in love, wisdom, clarity, discernment, and self-control. Moreover, it helps us to develop a personal relationship with the Lord.

Previously, we learned that we need God—His Spirit and His presence—as much as we need food, water, and air (air being the most equivalent). We overpower the flesh by staying connected to God and intentionally being led by the Spirit of God *(Galatians 5:22-25).* It's near impossible to overpower the flesh if we are far from God's voice, guidance, and influence because the voices of darkness and the temptations of this world are far too loud and plentiful. Sin separates us from God which is why obedience is *the key.*

Having a close relationship with God and spending time with Him regularly is what strengthens you spiritually. Reading the Word and learning about the type of person Jesus was is how you get to know and fall in love with Him. Once you develop a personal relationship with the Lord and fall in love with Him, you will no longer be indifferent, feel comfortable, or have peace with disobeying Him because this grieves Him and you now have a totally different relationship and bond with Him. You will understand that sin is harmful to you and others, and you will no longer want to hurt God, yourself, or others in this way.

Once you see Him change you from the inside out and give you power over the flesh, which has held you captive and in dysfunction for years, you will have experienced the power, presence, and existence of God. What follows next will be the discovery of your purpose and your spiritual gifts. God has so much in store for you!

Just remember to be diligent. The simple key is to care more about what God thinks than anyone or anything else. *This* is the true definition of putting God first. You have to be serious about your relationship with God and be willing to stick with Him no matter what. Loyalty. You won't find great results if you are lukewarm and 'on and off' with your pursuit of a real relationship with Him. It's important to spend time getting to know the Lord *every day*. This means cutting out some other activities that tie up your time but have no true value or ability to transform you and your life; for example, too much TV or social media.

Improving your life begins with improving yourself, particularly your heart.

Now that I've said all of that, let's read the scriptures below, which substantiate everything we've just discussed.

"I advise you to obey only the Holy Spirit's instructions. He will tell you where to go and what to do, and then you won't always be doing the wrong things your evil nature wants you to. For we naturally love to do evil things that are just the opposite from the things that the Holy Spirit tells us to do; and the good things we want to do when the Spirit has his way with us are just the opposite of our

natural desires. These two forces within us are constantly fighting each other to win control over us, and our wishes are never free from their pressures. When you are guided by the Holy Spirit you need no longer **force** yourself to obey Jewish laws."
Galatians 5:16-18 TLB

Characteristics of the Flesh

"But when you follow your own wrong inclinations your lives will produce these evil results: impure thoughts, eagerness for lustful pleasure, idolatry, spiritism (that is, encouraging the activity of demons), hatred and fighting, jealousy and anger [fits of rage], constant effort to get the best for yourself, complaints and criticisms, the feeling that everyone else is wrong except those in your own little group—and there will be wrong doctrine, envy, murder, drunkenness, wild parties, and all that sort of thing. Let me tell you again as I have before, that anyone living that sort of life will not inherit the Kingdom of God."
Galatians 5:19-21 TLB

Characteristics of the Spirit

"But when the Holy Spirit controls our lives he will produce this kind of fruit in us: love, joy, peace, patience, kindness, goodness, faithfulness, gentleness and self-control; and here there is no conflict with Jewish laws. Those who belong to Christ have nailed their natural evil desires to his cross and crucified them there. If we are living now by the Holy Spirit's power, let us follow the Holy Spirit's leading in every part of our lives."
Galatians 5:22-25 TLB

Be sure to take a look at *John 14:15-28* which tells us more about the Father, the Son, and the Holy Spirit.

Does This Really Work Though?

Absolutely. I wouldn't encourage you to do something that I don't follow, do, and practice in my own life. If I couldn't do it and if it didn't work for me, it wouldn't be worth sharing. I'm writing this book because I know what it's like to have questions, confusion, and unfulfillment in life, and I know what it's like to put an end to that type of existence.

I came to a point in life where, after experiencing the same frustrations over and over, I had enough of dysfunction, darkness, and defeat. I had enough of trying to do it my way and trying to figure it out on my own. I soon realized that all of the answers and direction I needed had been right in front of me and within grasp all along.

Some may think that living a life of obedience is like being in a boring jail. But the truth is, a life of obedience is freedom. Living in sin is more like prison because you're constantly doing things that are opposite of what you know and wish you could be doing. A life of obedience allows you to live your best life—the life God has for you. It makes you into a person you actually love, respect, and enjoy living with. Living in obedience gives us self-control, which is a fruit of the Spirit. Imagine being in control of yourself, or having a designated driver (DD) who ensures your safety while you relax. You can trust your DD, and pretty soon you can trust yourself again.

Knowing better yet not doing better, I had been there and done that. I'd had enough. That was when I was ready and willing to leave the "crowd" mentality and be **in** the world but not **of** it. As the Word of God transformed my mind and opened my eyes, I became the sober person at the party (in the world). I could see people doing the same counterproductive things over and over and over, like I used to.

I was happy to leave that world, and I don't miss it. My life became all about God and none about me. When it came to matters of the heart, I didn't want to call the shots anymore because that usually led to disappointment, and the end result was never worth it. Also, I don't like temporary gain nor temporary satisfaction. I like the real deal—the good stuff that doesn't perish or fade. That stuff comes from God and *only* God.

My discontent with a series of toxic and dysfunctional events led me to God, and obedience led me into a life of fulfillment, peace, joy, and happiness. It led me to becoming the woman I've always wanted to be and living the life I've always wanted to live— a meaningful one.

I wrote this book because everyone wants to know how they can find happiness. Everyone is looking for answers and peace. I found it by doing the one thing that no one does: *listen*. Just listen to Him. God's voice is the only one that matters. Not your boss', not your spouse's, not your friends', and not even your voice because your voice might be saying, "Let's get wasted!" I'm kidding. But seriously, the only voices that matter are the ones that are aligned with God's Word.

I know this will help some, and others will decide not to leave worldly things behind. They love it too much and are willing to accept the losses that come with it for temporary gains. Many want to get happiness and fulfillment their way, not God's way, which is why they never find it. Every man makes his own decisions, and I judge not. I'm only sharing what I know. God will call, few will answer.

There are a lot of religions out there. But I don't know of another one that has a Savior who guarantees salvation for you when this life is over simply through faith and love, which is what the world needs. Love is the one thing in this world that there's just too little of. One of my favorite songs by the way.

If you are reading this and you're in a place similar to where I was, or you just feel it in your heart that you are ready to leave the old you behind and start new, this prayer is for you:

Dear Heavenly Father,
Thank You for never giving up on me. Thank You for giving me a chance to hear Your call and happily accept. Thank You God for sending Your only begotten Son to die on the cross for my sins. Heavenly Father, I accept Jesus Christ as Lord and Savior of my life. Heavenly Father, I ask that You forgive me of all of my sins, and I thank You for Your forgiveness and for Your grace. Thank You, Lord, that I am new and made whole today by Your loving kindness, and I pray that You will create a right spirit in me. I welcome the Holy Spirit into my heart. Lord, I pray that You will examine my heart and remove anything that You find to be unclean. Give me a clean heart, Lord. Help and lead me to love You, myself, and others. Give me a desire to seek You and Your presence daily, and above all, Lord, let no opinion in this world matter more to me than Your opinion. Remove all selfishness and pride

from my heart, Lord, in the Name of Jesus. Protect me from the enemy and all of his tricks and schemes as I seek to strengthen my faith and walk with You. Give me faith and endurance to stick with You and to stand fervently through all tests and trials. Order my steps from today and forevermore. Lord, I believe that Jesus laid down His life for me and was raised from the dead by You three days later. Lord, I pray that You remove all doubt from my heart, and silence the voice of the enemy when he attempts to destroy my faith and relationship with You. Father, I pray for wisdom. Father, I pray for discernment. Father, I believe that the blood of Jesus and the power of the Holy Spirit are mighty enough to wash all my sins away and remove all darkness from my heart and from my life. Father, today, I am saved by faith. Today I am forgiven, and the things of the past matter no more. Thank You for giving me a new start. Thank You for hearing my prayer.

I love You, and I thank You. In Jesus' Name.

Amen

End-of-Chapter Reflection

Chapter 8
Why We Do the Things We Do

1. In life, we either do good and wise things or bad and foolish things. What is the underlying factor behind why we do the things we do?

_____

_____

_____

_____

_____

_____

_____

2. What are your biggest takeaways from Chapter 8?

_____

_____

_____

_____

_____

_____

_____

_____

_____

_____

3. How will you incorporate what you learned from Chapter 8 into your life today (and moving forward)?

_____

_____

_____

_____

_____

_____

_____

_____

_____

_____

_____

4. Name something new that you discovered about yourself.

_____

_____

_____

_____

_____

_____

_____

_____

5. Name something new or interesting that you learned about God, life, and/or people.

_____

_____

_____

_____

_____

_____

_____

6. Journal any other notes, takeaways, or reminders that you'd like to capture from Chapter 8.

_____

_____

_____

_____

_____

_____

_____

_____

_____

_____

_____

_____

_____

_____

_____

_____

_____

Chapter 9

Why Some Choose Not to Believe
Part One

There are a few reasons many have chosen not to believe or have lost their faith in God. It could be because they didn't get their way or something or someone they really wanted, or because they got hurt by people who claimed to be Christians or in the church. In many cases, it's due to pain or disappointment that comes from someone we love. Maybe they abused us in some way or abandoned us, and maybe we did nothing to deserve it. Or maybe we loved someone dearly, they passed away, and we got mad at God in return. "Why would God do this if He loves me?" some might say. Other reasons some have chosen not to believe or obey is because they don't understand God, and in some cases, it's simply due to FOMO, fear of missing out. "If I follow and obey Jesus then I can't do this and that anymore!" some say.

As you can see, there are several different reasons some people in the world have either lost their faith or have chosen not to believe in God at all. This is what we will be discussing in this insightful and eye-opening chapter.

In the next chapter, we will be learning a new way to perceive and address the pain and loss we experience in life. In this chapter, we will be discussing the following bullet points and reasons why some have shaky or non-existent faith:

- Hurt by, let down, or deceived by people (including godly pretenders/false prophets/phonies)
- Can't understand God
- Not getting their way (i.e. losing something they had or never getting something they wanted)
- Fear of missing out (FOMO)
- What others may think

I decided it was pertinent to include this chapter because, as expressed throughout this book, I've discovered that faith and obedience to God is *the answer* and cure to rectifying a dysfunctional life. As a matter of fact, through experience, observation, and examination, I've concluded that unbelief and disobedience to God is the *direct* cause of a dysfunctional life. However, I understand that, for most, accepting this rationale is easier said than done.

Therefore, I wanted to address several life situations that can or have caused people to lose their faith so we can get ahead of this derailment and not allow the temporary trials and disappointments of life to become a permanent and lifelong problem. In order to navigate life triumphantly, we must have a healthy and adequate understanding, perspective, and response when it comes to disappointment, pain, and loss.

The truth is, we only have two options when it comes to pain, loss, and disappointment. We can turn sour about it and allow the bad times to dominate our path in a negative way—or, we can take the advice written in this book and other similar teachings and see pain for what it's worth and what it's meant to do in our lives, as well as what it's *not* meant to do.

As mentioned in Chapter 2 "The Purpose of Life," we get so upset about what happens to us in this temporary place when all along, it has nothing to do with us or our personal preferences to begin with. Our time on this earth is *not* about us. It just isn't. *That* is where many are mistaken. Life is so much bigger than us. Our life is not our own *(1 Corinthians 6:19)*.

Everything that happens to us has a purpose and will somehow prepare, lead, and align us to fulfill our God-given purpose. This only happens when we are able to adopt the proper perspective of loss and pain.

When we can wrap our minds around the fact that life is not about us, then we can stop taking everything so personally when it comes to our short time on this earth. Yes, in the world we will have trials *(John 16:33)*, God tells us this. Yes, rain falls on the just *and* the unjust *(Matthew 5:45)*. But what does God say about it in *John 16:33*? *"Take heart, I have overcome the world."* In other words, He's saying, "Don't worry, I've got this!" I love how our Father lets us know exactly what to expect in this world and exactly what to do, as well as taking our hand (if we allow) and walking with us, right through it!

Now, without further ado, let's jump into the first, highly common bullet point and reason that some find it difficult to or have chosen not to believe.

Reason 1
People, False Prophets, Phonies, and Godly Pretenders

I have found that far too many people in the world have turned away from God due to people and their actions. I once heard a great quote:

> *"If being hurt by the church causes you to lose faith in God, then your faith was in people, not God."*
> *— Unknown*

God directs our paths and tells us how to escape the pitfalls and traps set before us by the adversary. All we really have to do is, not just hear but apply the wisdom provided to us by our Father. For God says to not just be hearers of the word, but doers *(James 1:22-25)*. We cannot lose when we obey God and follow His commands. They truly are protection and, as proven over and over again, they are the roadmap to triumph and prosperity.

In this next verse, God teaches and instructs us NOT to put our trust in man. Understanding and applying this principle makes *all* the difference in the world.

> *"It is better to trust in the LORD than to put confidence in man."*
> *Psalms 118:8 KJV*

If we obeyed this wise command and guidance from God, it would save us from so much heartache, pain, and disappointment in our lives because, if you think about it, the number one thing people crave and live to acquire is the very thing that causes the most heartache and pain in our lives: *relationships*.

Humans are deeply flawed, we know that. We're not perfect and we all make mistakes. Only God is perfect, and only God is the perfect embodiment of true love. *That* is why He cautions and directs us to ONLY put our trust in Him. He knows that we will only end up hurt if we put our trust in and make idols of man.

Many people find themselves in heartbreaking and detrimental situations from not applying this one commandment to their lives. As human beings, we know that we put our trust in people all the time and end up being let down. Therefore, it's easy to see that this is a wise and relevant command. It's also easy to see how this guidance helps and protects us if we actually apply it, same as every other commandment.

We are created to seek God and *His* purpose for our lives. We were *not* created to seek the validation of other human beings or material possessions. God wants us to know that *He* is all we need. When we do what He designed and created us to do, which is to put Him first, everything else is added to us and falls into place *(Matthew 6:33)*.

Many people in society today don't like the idea of following commands or being "commanded" to do anything. It puts a bad taste in their mouths. If this is you and this is something that affects your psyche and ability to obey God, don't look at it solely as commandments, per se. Look at God's commandments as Laws of Protection and Direction. That's precisely what they are.

Following God's commandments, or Laws of Protection and Direction, leads us to *not* put our trust in man. Our adherence would protect us from false prophets. It would protect us from those who come to use and abuse us and those who smile in our faces but have evil intentions. We should love and respect one another, but we don't owe our trust to everyone. Trust is something that is earned. Giving it away freely and opening yourself up to being manipulated and abused by people isn't wise.

Many people in the world have become upset with God because of pain inflicted upon them by someone. In other words, many have allowed a human being, who *does not* follow, honor, nor listen to God, to turn them away from God. God commands us to love Him and to love others, period. If someone truly hurt you, it's likely they disobeyed God. They did what THEY wanted to do, not what God commanded them to. Correspondingly, God encourages us to continue in obedience and leave revenge to Him. He assures us each person will pay for the wrong they've done *(Romans 2:6).*

There are false prophets in the world, people who actually hate God but pretend to be led by God in order to turn others away from Him.

> *"Beware of false prophets who come disguised as*
> *harmless sheep but are really vicious wolves."*
> *(Matthew 7:15 NLT, Jesus' own words)*

Take a look at *Matthew 7:15-23* to learn more about false prophets, godly pretenders, and how to identify them. They make you trust them by pretending to be good, and then they behave disgustingly and commit an ungodly act (lying or hurting you or someone else), hence turning the injured party away from God. We see this time and time again.

For this reason, in the next chapter I included a section describing what a true Christian looks like and how to identify a good person. There are just some things good people don't do. It goes against every fiber of their being. It goes against their nature and who they are. Respectively, we have to pay attention to people's behaviors and protect our hearts accordingly.

Always remember that just as you have chosen to be a loving person to someone, they could very well make the same decision. And if they choose to do the opposite, remember, at the end of the day, people will be who *they* decide to be, not who *you* wish they would be or who God wants them to be. We can't want better for others. They have to want it for themselves.

I'm not saying we aren't supposed to love and pray for them; we are. But we aren't supposed to knowingly and willingly open ourselves and our hearts to be trampled over, allowing our self-worth, self-esteem, peace, and joy to be shattered by those who have displayed that they do not *choose* to *truly* and accurately love us in accordance with God's will, the right way *(1 Corinthians 13)*.

Reason 2
Can't Understand God

"Trust in the LORD with all your heart, and lean not on your own understanding. Seek His will in all you do, and He will show you which path to take." - Proverbs 3:5-6 NLT

Some don't believe because they don't understand. The Lord tells us in Isaiah 55:8 KJV, *"For my thoughts are not your thoughts, neither are your ways my ways."*

As we've discussed, God created us all—each of us—for a specific purpose and reason. However, we, as humans, are not intellectually capable of understanding all that God is doing and why. As a child, did you always understand what your parents were doing, and telling you, and why? Probably not. You were not mature enough, you hadn't lived long enough, and you did not have the whole picture. You were not on a mental or intellectual level that was capable of understanding what your parents were doing and why. They knew things that you didn't know and wouldn't understand until later in life.

> *"In the same way, we can see and understand only a little about God now, as if we were peering at His reflection in a poor mirror; but someday we are going to see Him in His completeness, face to face. Now all that I know is hazy and blurred, but then I will see everything clearly, just as clearly as God sees into my heart right now."*
> 1 Corinthians 13:12 TLB

It's no different for us as children of God. God will not do anything to hurt us. However, He will correct us, out of love, when necessary *(Job 5:17)*. In actuality, God deserves all respect and reverence because He *is* good. All He asks is for us to reverence Him, and to love and be kind to one another. Just like any good parent tells their kids. As a parent, would you be okay with your child disrespecting you and disobeying you? No.

The world has this double standard. Many feel they should be able to do whatever they want, make their own rules—good or bad—and still get their way. Some go so far as to believe they should still be immensely blessed regardless of their behavior. This is preposterous. We shouldn't look at God's parenting any differently from our own.

Considering the fact that life is not about us, God will allow things to happen that will equip us for and nudge us toward the path we were designed for and called to. Will we always understand? Of course not. Not always. But you only know this when you read the Bible for yourself and develop your own *personal* relationship with God. *This* is the most important thing in life. This is when it all begins to make sense. And finally, this is why God advises us to seek wisdom. He tells us clearly where to find it *(Proverbs 9:10 and Proverbs 4:6-13)*.

Although every Word of God equips us with wisdom, the entire book of Proverbs is dedicated toward the specific teaching of wisdom.

"If any of you lack wisdom, ask God, who gives it generously to all, and it will be given to you. But when you ask Him, you must believe and not doubt, for a person with divided loyalty is as unsettled as a wave of the sea that is blown and tossed by the wind. Such people should not expect to receive anything from the Lord."
James 1:5-7

Through the wisdom of God, you can receive clarity in life and literally avoid the typical snares that lead so many into dysfunction.

Generally speaking, you can and will not understand *everything* about anything. So, why waste time and energy worrying about things that will take a lifetime to figure out, will never be figured out, or are just too far beyond human comprehension? There is *One* who knows all—the Holder of infinite wisdom—are we not better off to simply trust in Him?

The problem is, many people strain themselves trying to understand God's ways and His plans even though He says, "*...lean not to your own understanding*," and "*...my ways are not your ways.*"

I don't fully understand how WiFi or the internet works. In fact, there are many other inventions in this world that I may never completely understand, yet I utilize and benefit from these amazing creations every day. I don't have to understand 100 percent how it works in order to utilize and benefit from it.

I understand that a mind far greater than mine in this area of expertise understands how it works, and that's good enough for me. We don't 100 percent know the outcome for many decisions we face. It could be choosing a college, accepting a new job in another city, or starting a family. We don't always have all of the answers beforehand, but we know *enough* to determine the best way to go. However, for some reason, people expect to have 100 percent understanding about the two most impenetrable subjects in existence: *God and creation.*

Humans have created many amazing things—cellphones, computers, spaceships, and more. However, these things are man-made, and man is *not* the highest intelligence nor the highest power. The Highest Power created the sun and the moon and the seas. He not only made them, He sustains them, and He has since the beginning of time. The Highest Intelligence knows things that humans don't know and created things that humans can't create, from nothing. This Higher Being is God.

Can humans create the sun, life, people, animals, water, air, or trees? Can humans make sure the sun remains in place for thousands of years and doesn't burn everyone and everything up by accidentally getting just a little too close? I could go on and on about everything God knows and has created. If man can create great things that aren't easy to explain or understand, how much more magnificent and complicated are the things of God and His creation?

Some people don't want to go through life believing in something that they feel may not be true or real, but as I mentioned in Chapter 5, from their viewpoint there are *only* two outcomes. Either God is real and everything He said in the Bible is true, or it's not, and who knows 100 percent? It's 50/50, from that viewpoint. All we can do is make the *best* decision based on what we DO know about life as it correlates to God's Word, not based on what we don't know. The truth is, it's the most important choice we'll ever make because our life depends on it, literally.

Having said that, don't get too wrapped up in the "hard to understand" aspects of God because, truth be told, there are far more straightforward things that we CAN see, understand, and experience in the Bible that are evident in everyday life.

Not understanding *everything* about God right now is normal *(1 Corinthians 13:12),* and it's okay, because He has given us more than enough information, direction, keys, and wisdom to triumph abundantly in life.

Unfortunately, the masses give more weight to the ambiguities of God and life instead of progressing from that which we *can* feel, sense, grasp, and apply. As long as you shy away from the thought patterns and ways of the world, you can be sure to experience a better quality of life.

Reason 3
Hard Times

Many people find themselves angry and upset with God because they have experienced hard times, weren't dealt the best hand, and either lost or didn't get something they wanted in life. We talk more about this in the next chapter!

An important thing for us to remember and understand is that the devil is good at using people and the trials of life to turn us against God. This is his number one goal and tactic, and—unfortunately—he has a pretty hefty success rate. I believe it's important for us to discuss this topic because turning against God is the one thing you don't ever want to do in any circumstance.

Reading the Bible is paramount because it privies us to the tricks of the devil and the tactics he uses in aims of defeating us and bringing us down. If you're living a dysfunctional life, there's a good chance you've been falling for the tricks, plots, and schemes of the enemy. God and the wisdom in His Word are what cause us to be too wise for the devil to fool or to be led into a life of dysfunction and defeat.

Understanding and correctly handling the hard times and pain that we face makes all the difference in the overall journey, quality, and outcome of our lives. If God allows you to go through it, He can and will use it to prosper you, and He will repay you, many times over, in joy for any loss or pain you suffer—that is, when you continue to trust Him even through the bad times *(1 Peter 1:6-7)*.

This scripture tells us that God, at times, will test our faith. It's easy to believe in God when everything is going our way, but what about when it's time to go through the fire, the hurt, and the pain? Will you go through it with God, trusting Him to walk with you and lead you out of it not even smelling of smoke *(Daniel 3:27)*? Or will you turn from God and go through life's fires on your own, burning the whole way with pain that doesn't seem to ever go away?

I heard a powerful message one day which stated that God doesn't always want to take us out of the fire. Sometimes He is trying to make us fireproof. The messenger had a suggestion for us when we face trials. He recommended that we invite God into the fire with us instead of asking Him to take us out. I thought this was a powerful and interesting perspective because there is a popular phrase that says, "What doesn't kill you makes you stronger."

Maybe you are going through the fire right now because God is preparing you for something ahead that requires you to withstand temperatures of up to 400 degrees. This trial is equipping you for that. Maybe what you are going through right now is equipping you to be strong enough and resilient enough to fulfill the purpose for which you were called and created.

In life, there are two kinds of people: those who let hard times get the best of them, and those who don't. The majority allow hard times to determine the entire course of their lives. Few allow hard times to be just what they are: *temporary*.

We don't always need to change our circumstances; sometimes we just need to change the way we see them. Perspective is everything. Wisdom is everything. And wisdom comes from where? You got it. God and His Word.

Again, I have to reiterate, life isn't about us. It just isn't. It is bigger than us and what we want. Think about it. How many humans do you know who want things that are worthwhile? Or do they mostly crave earthly, materialistic things that don't really matter at the end of time?

Jesus was sent to Earth for a purpose, and that purpose was *not* to sow His royal oats! In other words, He didn't come here to have a ball and do every crazy and destructive thing He could think of…which some call "fun." Like us, He came to this "not always pleasant" world temporarily and for a specific reason. He was a perfect man who was falsely accused, spit on, hated, and unjustifiably crucified by evil men; and He is the Son of God! What makes anyone think WE are supposed to walk through this life or this world unscathed?

Some people get so mad at God after they go through certain things. When this happens, it causes a domino effect of hard times. The individual perpetuates a lifetime of heartache for themselves by allowing the enemy to convince them to turn on God. This demise is avoided when you trust and understand that God will always turn around anything meant for your harm and use it for your good *(Genesis 50:20)*. But you have to stick with Him and trust His divine plan for you in order to receive what He has for you.

A few of my favorite examples to use when it comes to NOT allowing hard times to take you away from God's will for you are the stories of Jesus, Martin Luther King, Jr. (MLK), and Joseph from the book of Genesis. Most of us know the history of Jesus and MLK. They fulfilled their purpose, despite the trials and tribulation of this world, and their names, work, and honor lives on. We see their continuous impact on the world, no matter how much time has passed since they walked this earth.

These examples show men who were faced with discouraging trials, yet they did not let those trials take them off the path for which they were called and destined. I also highly recommend a book titled, *The Alchemist* by Paulo Coelho. Likewise, this book provides an amazing example of the reward in persisting through tough times!

Have you gotten around to reading the story of Joseph yet *(Genesis chapters 37-50)*? If not, remember to do so! This story is a great example of how to prevail in times where most would give up. It demonstrates how God will work everything out for the good of those who love the Lord *(Romans 8:28)*. When you look at these stories, and the stories of many others, did their enemies really win in the end? Not at all.

> *"For His Holy Spirit speaks to us deep in our hearts, and tells us that we really are God's children. And since we are His children, we will share His treasures—for all God gives to His Son Jesus is now ours too. But if we are to share His glory, we must also share His suffering. Yet what we suffer now is nothing compared to the glory He will give us later."*
> *Romans 8:16-18 TLB*

Imagine how differently the lives and impact of these great men would've turned out had they given up on God, goodness, and their purpose. God will always make everything you experience—good or bad—worthwhile when you trust and believe in Him unwaveringly.

Once we're able to wrap our minds around the fact that life is not about us or what we want, we will be able to view disappointment and loss differently. Once we understand this, we'll find that God has a plan far greater and far beyond anything we could ever think, hope, or imagine *(Ephesians 3:20)*.

When you turn your back on God, you block your ability to heal. This is called being "broken." How does something operate when it is broken? It malfunctions. It does not operate correctly, efficiently, or sufficiently. This is what happens to any person who has not taken the time to heal and who is living a life detached from God.

That is why it's so imperative to know God and His Word on a personal and intimate level. If you know God and His Word, you'll understand that anything God allows you to go through, He WILL turn it around and use it for your good, to prosper you. If you don't understand what I'm saying, it's simply because His ways and His greatness often exceed human comprehension and expectation.

Reason 4

Fomo

Fear of Missing Out

There's a vast number of people in the world who refuse to believe in or obey God due to Fear of Missing Out or FOMO. God's commandments go against the iniquitous nature and desires of human flesh. Therefore, many feel as though they are missing out if they actually follow and obey God. For example, this would mean you can't have sex with whoever you want whenever you want. Well, let's break this down and examine this. What are you missing out on? In this case, you're missing out on sexually transmitted diseases, unwanted pregnancies, failed relationships, broken homes, heartbreak, porn addiction, and many other problems that stem from having our own approach to sex instead of God's. This is a seed that leads to mounds of related dysfunction and destruction in the lives of human beings.

When it comes to FOMO, are you really missing out on anything? The answer is no; besides temporary pleasure, which pays in lifelong dividends of dysfunction, lack, and long-term disappointment. You don't have to take my word for it. We see this everyday. God tells us not to fornicate for our own good and protection, not to punish us.

There's a right and a wrong way to do things in life and that's just the way it is. If you want a good and less dysfunctional life, you have to understand these core concepts and how they free us from the typical life of darkness, self-destruction, and defeat.

Every sin is self-destructive. Besides temporary pleasure with long-term pain, we benefit in no way from sin. Sin causes more problems than benefits, and the temporary pleasure it brings is never worth the true cost it incurs. FOMO is a huge reason many don't submit to God's will, but we've learned that an obedient life led by the Holy Spirit gives us much more to look forward to than a sinful life led by the flesh.

It's interesting to me how people fear missing out on the same dysfunctional experiences and outcomes they've been having all of their lives, but they don't fear missing out on what it's like to truly know God, to have His favor, to experience all of His promises, and to live a truly happy and fulfilled life. Why is it that no one seems to fear missing out on that?

Reason 5
What Others Think

Another major reason many choose not to believe is due to fear of being the odd man out. If you're concerned about what others think, you'd be more comfortable fitting in with the crowd. Being happy and fulfilled in life means being who God wants you to be, not who others want you to be.

When you want to elevate, this often means you may have to leave some people behind because not everyone around you wants to elevate with you. So, your options are simple: elevate and escape dysfunction, or don't elevate and stay with the crowd. Being afraid to step out and make your own path is something that keeps a lot of people trapped in misery, from becoming their best selves, and from living their best lives. It's far better to be the one who steps outside of your comfort zone and inspires others to do the same, to do better, and to be better. You can be the one others look up to and the breath of fresh air that other people so desperately need.

"Be the change you wish to see in the world."
- Gandhi

End-of-Chapter Reflection

Chapter 9
Why Some Choose Not to Believe
Part One

1. What are your biggest takeaways from Chapter 9?

_____

_____

_____

_____

_____

_____

_____

_____

2. How will you incorporate what you learned from Chapter 9 into your life today (and moving forward)?

_____

_____

_____

_____

_____

_____

_____

_____

3. Name something new that you discovered about yourself (if applicable).

_____

_____

_____

_____

_____

_____

_____

_____

_____

4. Name something new or interesting that you learned about God, life, and/or people.

_____

_____

_____

_____

_____

_____

5. Journal any other notes, takeaways, or reminders that you'd like to capture from Chapter 9.

_____

_____

_____

_____

_____

_____

_____

_____

Chapter 10

Why Some Choose Not to Believe
Part Two

Putting Pain into Perspective

I n the previous chapter, we discussed several reasons a person may have lost their faith and turned away from God. Most of the problems that we face in life are avoidable and are due to our own disobedience and unwise choices. However, on the other hand, there are trials we encounter in life which are no fault of our own. This is the type of pain we will be discussing in this chapter. If pain has hindered your life and your faith in God, allow me to share with you a new and healthy perspective of pain.

We know from experience that pain is temporary.

"Weeping may endure for a night, but joy cometh in the morning."
Psalms 30:5 NIV

Sickness, losing the life of someone we love, and being violated, abandoned, or abused by another human being are trials that fall on the just and on the unjust alike. In this world, a degree of pain, suffering, and loss are unavoidable *(John 16:33, Matthew 5:45)*. We may not understand why it has to be this way, but since there's no way around it—we definitely need to understand how to overcome pain instead of being consumed by it.

An important thing to realize is that God ensures we will be well compensated for our pain and suffering—that is, when we choose to *trust* Him through it all *(2 Corinthians 4:17-18), Romans 8:16-18)*. The problem is, many people don't understand how to perceive pain and loss through God's eyes. You may not be able to have that thing back or that person you lost, but God can and will bring back the joy you felt when that person or thing was around. If you were unfairly and severely hurt by someone, you can have the joy and peace back that you once had.

Some people don't allow this to happen. Instead, they allow that pain to negatively direct the course of their lives. There's a time and place for everything, and after excruciating pain and loss, there's definitely a time for mourning and weeping. As a matter of fact, don't skip this step. Mourn, be sad, face the pain, handle it, get it all out; and then, afterwards, allow the healing process to move forward.

A number of people get stuck. Maybe some don't want to get past it, maybe some just don't know how. Maybe they feel guilty for moving on and being happy again, or maybe they spend more time focusing on what they've lost rather than on what they still have and someday will have. Either way, we can absolutely move past the pain and be happy again; even happier than we were beforehand. But do we allow this to happen? Do we allow God to show us that He means it when He says:

"Many are the afflictions of the righteous,
but the LORD delivers him out of them all."
Psalms 34:19 NKJV

God doesn't do anything to harm us. Because of life's trials, this concept isn't easy for most to understand. However, God has a plan that is far beyond anything we can comprehend. As we know, this thing called life is bigger than us and what *we* want. When we make the mistake of quitting or getting mad at God for the way life goes, we end up prolonging the pain and suffering. We then go down a path of darkness that prevents us from experiencing all God has for us because—well, now we don't like Him or want anything to do with Him anymore—and remember, He doesn't force Himself on us.

God promises we will prevail when we trust Him through it all. *Not* when we decide to give up on Him, hate Him, or do it our way. God clearly tells us what to do and what *not* to do in any situation we face. *That's* what we need to remember if we truly want to thrive and be happy in this life, against all odds.

"So be truly glad. There is wonderful joy ahead, even though you
must endure many trials for a little while. These trials will show
that your faith is genuine. It is being tested as fire tests and purifies
gold—though your faith is far more precious than mere gold. So
when your faith remains strong through many trials, it will bring
you much praise and glory and honor on the day when Jesus
Christ is revealed to the whole world."
1 Peter 1:6-7 NLT

Life doesn't get better without God. It gets worse. That's why turning against God is the one thing you *never* want to do in any situation. The blessings and better days come when we stick with God and trust Him *through* the hard times. That's perseverance. That's faith.

Right now, you can probably imagine some things that once hurt but don't anymore. We may not be able to comprehend a miracle such as this, but as long as we don't make the mistake of adopting the wrong perspective of pain, we will always be better, stronger, and wiser after experiencing it. This is proof that God is in control and He does love us.

> *"'For I know the plans I have for you,' declares the Lord,*
> *'plans to prosper you and not to harm you,*
> *plans to give you hope and a future.'"*
> *Jeremiah 29:11 NIV*

Think about it like this. When you learned to crawl, walk, ride a bike, or skate, it seemed extremely hard at first, right? Wasn't it painful and frustrating when you fell down over and over? Yes, but you knew that was part of the process, and you knew that if you just kept enduring, you would conquer that feat. You *know* you will one day walk, skate, and ride a bike, even though it doesn't look or feel like you will in the moment.

> *"What is faith?*
> *It is the confident assurance that*
> *something we want is going to happen.*
> *It is the certainty that what we hope for is waiting for us,*
> *even though we cannot see it up ahead."*
> *Hebrews 11:1 TLB*

There are certain things you would never attempt to learn or do in life if you didn't see gain on the other side. Meaning, we *willingly* go through certain trials because we know there's a reward or something we want on the other side of that struggle. For example, we'll risk falling and scraping our knees and banging up our bodies when learning to ride a bike or skate. We'll exercise vigorously to the point where our bodies are sore because we know this will make us look and feel the way we desire after the pain subsides. We'll have surgery for an illness or get a vaccine shot because we know the pain won't be forever and we'll be better and stronger afterward. You get the point. We need to look at any and every type of pain in life the exact same way. No matter what type of pain you experience, there's always a benefit, a reward, and elevation on the other side when you have the proper perspective.

If you experience heartbreak or loss and you decide to become angry, bitter, and shut down, you are then mentally, emotionally, and spiritually incapable of progressing to a higher level, which is where your reward awaits; so the reward is delayed, if not voided.

You can now walk without stumbling. You can skate and ride a bike like a pro without a second thought. You progressed to another level, but it required you to have faith through frustration and believe that something good would come from it. Imagine if you had gotten upset because it hurt, and you walked away or quit. How could you ever elevate to the next level? Even though this example is quite simple, it's no different when we experience other unwarranted trials and pain. There will *always* be better days ahead when you apply these principles *(2 Corinthians 4:17)*.

In Chapter 3, we discussed the purpose of life. There are some trials in life that could be classified as "your cross to bear." Your "cross" is an unpleasant event or circumstance (sometimes more than one) that you must go through in order to fulfill your God-given purpose.

"I have told you these things, so that in me you may have peace.
<u>In this world you will have trouble</u>. But take heart!
I have overcome the world."
John 16:33 NIV

In this Bible verse, Jesus is letting us know, from His own mouth, that hard times are a part of life. Jesus, having lived in this world for 33 years, experienced it Himself.

Jesus was a perfect man who performed many miracles, helped many people, yet withstood terrible treatment. His miracles proved to many that He indeed was the Son of God, yet the hate in this temporary world led the jealous hearts of man to crucify Him. Jesus, the Son of God, an innocent man.

Now, let's put this all into perspective. From a human perspective, some might ponder, "Why would a loving God allow something like that to happen to His own child? Why bring a child into this world for this?"

In this example of Jesus' life, He suffered and experienced pain in this world even as the Son of God. Though our limited minds may not always understand God's purpose and plans, it's evident and proven that God will ALWAYS provide a reward many times greater than our pain and sacrifices *(Hebrew 5:8-9)*. This is something we will talk more about in Chapter 13.

*"Then Jesus said to them, 'You are such foolish, foolish people! You find it so hard to believe all that the prophets wrote in the Scriptures! Wasn't it clearly predicted by the prophets that the Messiah would have to **suffer all these things** <u>before entering his time of Glory</u>?'"*
Luke 24:25-26 TLB

Jesus trusted, obeyed, and fulfilled God's will. What was His reward?

*"What we are saying is this, Christ whose priesthood we have just described, is our High Priest, and is in heaven at the place of <u>greatest honor</u> **next to God himself.**"*
Hebrews 8:1 TLB

As far as perspective, I have a few questions for you. How long ago did Jesus live? Thousands of years ago? Correct. Who has never heard of Jesus? What is the best-selling book of all time? Who are we talking about right here and right now? Thousands of years later? That's right, Jesus. He lives and He reigns forever. Jesus is the most influential person who ever walked the face of this earth.

Now, does anyone refer to Jesus as a victim or a person that everyone feels sorry for? Or is He remembered for how great, kind, magnificent, and honorable He is? After the pain He suffered in the world, His reward was and still is the greatest reward of all, AND it's eternal.

My point is this: The pain that Jesus suffered in His short time on earth is NOT to be the focal point. Most people place way too much emphasis on the hard times they face and miss the big picture and their whole purpose for existing. I hope what you take from this is that there is a magnificent reward that is promised to you by God when you love, trust, obey, and fulfill the purpose *He* placed you here for. Pain in life is temporary, prosperous, and rewarding when interpreted correctly.

Let's take labor and childbirth for example.

> *"It will be the same joy as that of a woman in labor when her child is born—her anguish gives place to rapturous joy and the pain is forgotten."*
> *John 16:21 TLB*

When unwarranted pain is incorporated into your journey, it's necessary and in some way, it molds, shapes, leads, and prepares you for the purpose that the Creator put you here for.

I hope this bit of wisdom will prevent you from letting a temporary, painful situation rob you of your permanent and eternal place of honor and glory seated in the Kingdom of Heaven, which is promised and destined for you by God, your Creator, who loves you. Seek truth from God, our Father, not from this misguided, lost, and confused world.

> *"For His Holy Spirit speaks to us deep in our hearts, and tells us that we really are God's children. And since we are His children, we will share His treasures—*
> *for all God gives to His Son Jesus is now ours too.*
> *But if we are to share His glory, we must also share His suffering.*
> *Yet what we suffer now is nothing compared to the glory He will give us later."*
> *Romans 8:16-18 TLB*

If the devil can get you to adopt the wrong perception of pain, he can destroy you mentally, physically, spiritually, and ultimately.

> *"The thief comes only to steal and kill and destroy;*
> *I have come that they may have life,*
> *and have it to the full."*
> *John 10:10 NIV (Jesus' own words)*

Once you realize why we are here, you will not allow anything that happens in this world, including pain, to discourage and separate you from your Creator and the purpose He created and placed you here.

In this world, there will be trials and this is when your faith is tested. Again, it's easy to love and trust God when everything is going your way. If things don't go your way, will you respond as a child does? By pouting and rebelling against God, insisting that you have your way?

Wisdom is knowing that God, our Creator, knows what's best for us. He has the divine ability and has promised to work everything out for the good of those who love the Lord. Watch Him work. Don't let your pain and suffering be in vain. God has a divine plan and promise to prosper you and *"God is not a man, that He should lie" (Numbers 23:19 ESV)*. This doesn't mean you will always understand, right away, why you must experience certain things in your life, but understand that you can either allow it to take you backwards, to keep you stuck in place, or to propel you forward.

In accordance with *John 16:33*, we will undergo trials in this world—just make sure you don't go through all of this for nothing. Pain has the ability to birth some of our greatest blessings—like a pregnancy or near-death experience that wakes people up and changes their lives for the better. Don't miss out on your greatest blessing!

> *"Count it all joy, my brothers and sisters,*
> *whenever you face trials of many kinds,*
> *because you know that the testing of your faith*
> *produces perseverance. Let perseverance finish its*
> *work so that you may be mature and complete,*
> *not lacking anything."*
> *James 1:2-4 NIV*

End-of-Chapter Reflection

Chapter 10
Why Some Choose Not to Believe
Part Two

1. What are your biggest takeaways from Chapter 10?

_____

_____

_____

_____

_____

_____

_____

2. How will you incorporate what you learned from Chapter 10 into your life today (and moving forward)?

_____

_____

_____

_____

_____

_____

_____

_____

_____

3. Name something new that you discovered about yourself (if applicable).

_____

_____

_____

_____

_____

_____

_____

_____

_____

_____

_____

4. Name something new or interesting that you learned about God, life, and/or people.

_____

_____

_____

_____

_____

_____

5. Journal any other notes, takeaways, or reminders that you'd like to capture for Chapter 10.

_____

_____

_____

_____

_____

_____

_____

_____

Chapter 11

The Kind of Faith That Changes Everything

In this chapter, I'll be addressing a very important aspect of Christianity. There's a lot of confusion surrounding whether we are saved by faith alone or by faith *AND* works. Interestingly, there is scripture which seems to support both claims. So, what exactly must we do in order to be right with God? How do we *know* we have done enough—or that we *are* doing enough?

Parts of scripture profess we are saved by *faith alone,* not by works, while other parts declare faith without works is dead. So, which is it? How can we know if we are truly saved and what to do?

This is a very important topic, so I'm really happy to get into it and provide some clarity here. This area surely needs to be addressed because far too many people are confused when it comes to this subject. I used to be one of them.

"...faith is the substance of things hoped for,
the evidence of things not seen."
Hebrews 11:1 KJV

Faith vs. Works

The *entire* book of Galatians, specifically *Galatians 2:16*, is dedicated to making it clear that we are saved by faith alone, not by obeying laws. This book of the Bible really threw me for a loop. I was confused. I thought, *If all we have to do is believe, then the New Testament should be fairly short. One page would do it!* I wondered, *How can we "just believe," do whatever we want, and be saved from eternal damnation?* That seemed far too easy. In fact, it didn't sound right. To me, it sounded like something the devil would say: "Yeah, sin all you want, you'll still go to heaven!" See what I mean?

Contrarily, I came across *James 2:18-21,* which reminds us that *just* believing there's one God isn't enough—even demons believe and tremble in terror. *Okay! Now that sounds about right!* I thought.

But what's with the opposite statements? Still, I was confused because *James 2:26* states, *"faith without works is dead,"* but Galatians express that we are saved by faith alone. So...which is it?

It's easy to see why so many are confused about this. So, let's break it down!

Okay, here it is! It's true. We are absolutely and unequivocally saved by faith and faith alone. But! Before you break out the champagne bottles, there is a major component that most people aren't aware of. Here's the eye-opening game changer: Faith is *not* "just believing" that there is one God. As we learned in *James 2:19*, even demons believe. This alone lets us know there's something more to faith than "just believing" that God exists.

The kicker is, there are two kinds of faith. But there's only one kind that saves. This kind of faith is the only one that matters, and it's the only one that makes a difference. There's "living" faith and "dead" faith. Living faith works through genuine love for Christ, and it changes you.

"...the only thing that counts is faith expressing itself through love."
Galatians 5:6 NIV

This makes sense and aligns with God's Word because we were created to love, and loving the Lord with all our heart, soul, and mind is the *first and greatest* commandment of all *(Matthew 22:37-38)*. If your faith isn't manifested by love for Christ, it's as good as dead. We learn what love looks like to God and how to grow in faith in a later section of this chapter.

Dead faith isn't faith working through love for Christ, and this kind of faith doesn't change you or anything you do. Like demons, they know God exists but they don't care. They don't love Him. Dead faith is what most people have—this kind of faith doesn't result in change, and it does not save you.

Therefore, when the Bible mentions faith, it's speaking of one kind—the kind that saves.

I must emphasize that faith *starts* with love for the Lord, but it includes and extends to love for ourselves and others. Jesus tells us in *Matthew 22:37-40 TLB* that these are the two greatest commandments of all and if we keep these two, we will find that we are keeping all others. The Bible makes it clear in *1 John 5:1-2* and *1 John 4:20-21* that love for God includes love for His children, and that he who says he loves God but hates his brother or sister is a liar. Therefore, again, it all boils down to love, with love for the Lord being number one, because God *is* love. If we don't know and love God, we can't truly love ourselves and others *(1 John 5:2)*.

We are saved by faith alone because anyone, including any sinner, can choose, ask for, and receive Jesus, anytime they choose, and become saved. Having a solid understanding of what faith really is, is a game changer.

As we learned in Chapter 8, in faith, we are not relying on our own strength to do right but on the Holy Spirit, who has taken over and changed our hearts. The Holy Spirit is what causes the sinner to delight in righteous living. The Holy Spirit creates a new heart, a new way, and new desires in us that make us *want* to love, honor, obey, and live for God. It makes us desire righteousness. It overpowers the flesh. At this point, you aren't doing every silly thing you want to do! Now, you aren't a slave to the flesh. You are *free* to love and be wise and good and prosperous, all for the glory of the One who loves you, saved you, and called you! You didn't have to do anything to receive salvation besides accepting Jesus as your Lord and Savior, welcoming Him into your heart, and allowing Him to change you. That's all it takes. You did not work for this! You just opened your arms and your heart to Jesus. You decided to get to know Him.

I can testify that this is so true and so real. I was in the world. I had no idea how I could or would become a person who completely obeyed God. It seemed borderline impossible. But I kept getting to know the Lord through His Word and prayer, and sure enough, He changed me in ways that revealed His power, His realness, and His truth. I'm shocked at the change He made in me. I am truly a new person, and, again, I had no idea how to do it. I just went to the Lord in submission and reverence, trusted Him, read His Word daily, applied it, and I began to grow and change into a whole new person. I'm the best version of myself that I've ever been. I'm the person I've always wanted to be, and I absolutely enjoy serving the Lord.

I'm living proof that the Holy Spirit will take over because I once had no desire to be a preacher, teacher, or anything similar. I just wanted to escape dysfunction, love God, keep to myself, and wait patiently for His return. That's it. But now, God has caused me to have a desire to serve and do things I never imagined I would do—the things that He called and created me to do. It's amazing.

One pivotal element that really helped me transition is that I was literally tired of the world and all it has to offer: hate, envy, jealousy, greed, lust, lies, confusion, misery—I could go on and on. I had enough of that world, and now I'm free from it. Those things are around me but not *in* me nor in my life. It's like having a piece of heaven on Earth. I escaped it all, glory to God, and you can too. You just have to want to.

Only a small number will make it to heaven because only a small number *want* to give their lives to God. Some people love the world too much, so they can never let it go. However, I want you to understand that holding on to the world means holding on to dysfunction, darkness, defeat, and everything this book is teaching you how to escape.

This doesn't mean that nothing bad will ever happen. Bad things happened to Jesus, but look at Him now. Victory is the future for those who answer the call. We talked about that in the previous chapter.

I mentioned that the entire book of Galatians declares we are saved by faith *alone*. Keep in mind, we learned that it's important to read an entire book of the Bible and know the *complete* stance and conclusion of the book in order to receive an accurate interpretation. Here's a prime example: Everything the book of Galatians says about being saved by faith *alone* could confuse someone who doesn't understand what faith truly is. However, if we read the entire book, we won't miss the conclusion and final stance of the passage in *Galatians 6:15* which states, it doesn't matter if we have been circumcised (an Old Testament Law); all that matters is if we have really been ***changed*** into new and different people. So, again, there you have it. A true, honest, and saving faith is one that changes you. *That* is how you, God, and others know your faith is real. Is the Holy Spirit dwelling inside of you and guiding you? *That* is the question.

If faith is all I need, where can I get some?

One thing I'm very happy to say is that all of these answers are right there for us in the Bible. Let's talk more about what God wants from us and how to achieve it!

Genuine faith in Jesus is what saves us and helps us change, so the first thing we must do is get faith. How do we get it? "*Faith comes by hearing and hearing by the Word of God*" (Romans 10:17). This means we have to *hear* the Word of God in order to get faith. We discussed the importance of reading God's Word for yourself because if you don't know God's Word for yourself, you won't know when or if you are being taught the wrong thing by a preacher or prophet.

"Dear friends, do not believe everyone who claims to speak by the Spirit. You must test them to see if the spirit they have comes from God. For there are many false prophets in the world."
1 John 4:1 NLT

We talked a little about this in Chapter 6. Jesus brings attention to the issue of false prophecy in *Matthew 7:15-23* and tells us what to look out for.

In acquiring faith, the first thing to do is begin working on your personal relationship with the Lord. Make a daily habit of talking to Him in prayer, every day, and reading the Bible. There isn't a set amount of how much you need to read each day. Read what you can, but start at the beginning of a book of the Bible and finish that entire book, for example: John, Mark, Acts, Romans, and so on. Again, you can download "Where to Begin" instructions at: www.LatinaNicholeSmith.com/free.

If you want or feel you need a pastor, pray for God to lead you to honorable preachers who know His Word and who teach it correctly. When I'm on YouTube looking for a good sermon, I ask God to lead me to the right videos, and He does. He will provide you with anything you ask for that is in line with His will. If your request brings you closer to Him and helps you be better, He will answer your request. Make sure any preacher you listen to preaches what the Bible says. You should always test their message by reading the Word and making sure it aligns. The Holy Spirit will guide you.

Anytime you don't understand something, ask God to help you understand, but don't get stuck on that one thing. In due time, the Lord will bring clarity. Just keep learning and growing. Focus on the things you *do* understand and apply them to your life. It will all come together as you learn and grow in Christ.

If you'd like a recommendation for a preacher to listen to, I like listening to Dr. Tony Evans of Oak Cliff Bible Fellowship and The Urban Alternative. Just remember, in all of your ways, acknowledge the Lord, look to Him, and He will direct your path *(Proverbs 3:6)*. Pray for discernment and wisdom. As long as you are seeking God and His guidance, He will lead you.

The Road to Heaven

Oftentimes, people want to know if they're going to heaven and what it takes to get there. There are several verses in the Bible that tell us what type of behavior will keep us from inheriting the Kingdom of God *(1 Corinthians 6:9-10, Galatians 5:19-21)*, so be sure to pay close attention to such scriptures.

We know that the Lord's number one commandment is for us to love Him with all our heart, mind, and soul *(Matthew 22:37-38)*. But what does love look like to God?

And Jesus said…

> *"If you love me, you will keep my commandments."*
> *John 14:15 ESV*

As we can see here, **God's love language is *obedience.*** Obedience is "The Special Sauce" because it is the ***master key*** to life. Now we know what "loving God" looks like to God.

"…Whoever has my commands and keeps them is the one who loves
me. The one who loves me will be loved by my Father, and
I too will love them and show myself to them."
John 14:21 NIV

It's very easy to see what matters most to God: *love. Truly* loving Him and others. Not just saying you do. For many, when it comes to God, love is merely a word rather than an action.

"Dear friends, let us practice loving each other, for love comes from
God and those who are loving and kind show that they are the
children of God, and that they are getting to <u>know</u> him better. But if
a person isn't loving and kind, it shows that he doesn't <u>know</u> God—
for God is love."
1 John 4:7-8 TLB

"'Not everyone who calls out to me,
'Lord! Lord!' Will enter the kingdom of heaven.
Only those who actually do
the will of my Father in heaven will enter.
On judgment day, many will say to me, 'Lord! Lord!
We prophesied in your name, and cast out demons in your name,
and performed many miracles in your name.'
But I will reply, '<u>I never knew you</u>. Get away from me,
<u>you who break God's laws</u>.'"
Matthew 7:21-23 NLT

Remember, this does not mean you have to be perfect and able to do this when you come to Christ. Again, when the Holy Spirit takes over, He gives you new desires, helps you do the will of God, and even changes you in a way that makes you love and *want* to do the will of God.

Just remember, if Jesus is your Lord—truly your Lord—this means you obey Him, you care what He thinks, and you look to Him for guidance in what to do and what not to do. If you don't care what Jesus says nor listen to Him, is He really Lord of your life? No.

We've already discussed the benefits of having an authority over our lives that wants the best for us and everyone around us.

In the previous Bible verse, the Lord said, "Depart from me, I never knew you." How can we be sure that we *know God*?

"And we can be <u>sure</u> that we <u>know him</u> if we obey His
commandments. If someone claims, 'I know God,' but doesn't obey
God's commandments, that person is a liar and is not living in the
truth. But those who obey God's Word truly show how completely
they love Him. <u>That</u> is how we <u>know</u> we are living in Him. Those
who say they live in God should live their lives as Jesus did."
1 John 2:3-6 NLT

Be sure to read *1 John Chapter 3* which provides an even deeper understanding of this. Below is a powerful verse from that chapter. How else can you be sure you *know* Him and whether or not you are a child of God?

"But if you keep on sinning,
it shows that you belong to the devil, who
since he first began to sin has kept steadily at it.
But the Son of God came to destroy these works of the devil.

The person who has been born into God's family
does not make a practice of sinning, because
now God's life is in him; so he can't keep on sinning,
for this new life has been born into him and <u>controls</u> him—
He has been born again.
So now we can tell who is a child of God
and who belongs to the devil."
1 John 3:8-10 NLT

The reason only a few will make it to heaven is the simple fact that most humans want to do what they want to do, even though doing what they want to do only brings them misery.

Most people choose the world and everything else over God. This is the only reason the road to heaven is narrow. It isn't that it can't be done because we receive the Highest Power, which overtakes us when we surrender. But people don't want to surrender to God. They simply don't want to let go of the world. They don't want to give their lives or themselves completely to God; the life that He gave them to use for good. They love the pleasures of the flesh, even though it's eating them alive. This doesn't have to be you. God wants you to come to Him. That's why He sent His disciples, to let you know He wants all of His children to choose Him; to choose love; to choose life.

"If you cling to your life, you will lose it;
but if you give up your life for me, you will find it."
Matthew 10:39 NKJV

"Jesus answered,
'I am the way, the truth, and the life…'"
John 14:6 NIV

Read the Bible story of the Prodigal Son. This story is a display of how much it means to God for His children to find their way back home to Him. Not the "perfect" children. God doesn't expect you to be perfect. He just wants you to come.

Solidifying Your Faith

Generally, we don't know how strong or real our faith really is until it's tested. Something that worked quite well for me was to imagine going through the worst—the absolute worst thing I could imagine in my life. How would I feel? What would I do? If you can say you would walk away from God, your faith isn't real. This is something we talk more about in the next chapter.

"They went out from us, but they did not really belong to us.
For if they had belonged to us, they would have remained with us;
But their going showed that none of them belonged to us."
1 John 2:19 NIV

We discussed always looking and thinking ten steps ahead. This helps to set yourself up for success and to keep you stable and on track. Hereby, it's imperative to think about consequences before they occur. This way, you can always be a few steps ahead and not taken aback or thrown off guard.

In the next chapter, we'll learn more about what a real, living, and saving faith consists of. Some people feel as though they are doing the right thing, but nothing is changing. Let's talk about a few reasons this might be, make a few tweaks, and turn this around! Because loving God the right way, which is His *number one* commandment, truly changes everything!

End-of-Chapter Reflection

Chapter 11
The Kind of Faith That
Changes Everything

1. What are the two major differences between "living" faith and "dead" faith?

_____

_____

_____

_____

_____

2. What is God's love language, the *master key* to life, and what do I call it (nickname)?

_____

3. What are your biggest takeaways from Chapter 11?

_____

_____

_____

_____

_____

_____

_____

_____

4. How will you incorporate what you learned from Chapter 11 into your life today (and moving forward)?

_____

_____

_____

_____

_____

_____

_____

5. Name something new that you discovered about yourself (if applicable).

_____

_____

_____

_____

_____

_____

_____

_____

_____

6. Name something new or interesting that you learned about God, life, and/or people.

_____

_____

_____

_____

_____

7. Journal any other notes, takeaways, or reminders that you'd like to capture from Chapter 11.

_____

_____

Chapter 12

Why Life Still Sucks
for Some Believers

I'm excited to dive into this chapter because there are *so* many believers in the world who are trying to figure out what they are doing wrong or what more they have to do in order to experience the promises of God: peace, fulfillment, happiness, and so on.

If you see this happening to others, or if this applies to you, and you feel like you love God and are a good person, yet life still sucks, the reason is likely one, or more, of the nine issues we are about to cover in this chapter.

Number 1
Not Truly Knowing What a Christian Is or What Being a Christian Really Means

Many people in the world, including many believers, don't truly understand what a Christian is and what being a Christian means.

Sadly, more and more people are beginning to look at Christianity as a joke because many people who call themselves Christians don't act much differently from people who aren't. This shouldn't be.

As mentioned throughout this book, everything we need to know about God, humans, and this thing called life can be found in the Bible, the instruction manual for life. So, when it comes to matters as significant as this, I rely on God for answers and I love how He provides us with answers as clear as this:

> *"And how can we be sure that we belong to him? By looking within ourselves: Are we really trying to do what he wants us to? Someone may say, 'I am a Christian; I am on my way to heaven; I belong to Christ.' But if he doesn't do what Christ tells him to, he is a liar. But those who do what Christ tells them to will learn to love God more and more. That is the way to know whether or not you are a Christian. Anyone who says he is a Christian should live as Christ did."*
> *1 John 2:3-6 TLB*

I must bring to your attention that we referenced this scripture in the previous chapter, "Road to Heaven" section, which describes how we can be sure we *know* God. In the previous chapter, I quoted the NLT version.

Take a moment to flip back and look at the NLT rendition of this scripture. Notice that the NLT, and other translations, replace the word *Christian* with "know Him." This implies that truly being a Christian means *knowing* God. Hence, on judgment day, a true Christian does *not* have to fear hearing the following words from the Lord, "Depart from me, I never *knew* you."

So, now we know the definition of a Christian. Now we know what Christianity looks like, what it means, and what it signifies. The believer who does not fully understand what it means to be a Christian doesn't realize, when they call themselves a Christian, others pay close attention to their behavior. When people see a "Christian" indulging in sin or acting with a lack of self-control and kindness, they ask themselves, "Why would I want to be anything like them or follow their God, if THAT is how they act?"

I'm not saying this to be judgmental in any way. I'm saying this only to bring awareness to a serious matter that many may not even have thought about.

We are to be *in* the world but not *of* it. It should always be easy for anyone to distinguish a Christian by the fruit of their actions and words—being genuinely set apart and Christ-like. The behavior of Christians should be "*that*" which brings others closer to God, not "*that*" which turns them away. Christians are to be an example and a light in this dark world. We are to be a vehicle for God to deliver miracles, light, and love—not a vehicle used by the adversary to stir up chaos, destruction, hate, pain, and confusion.

"But when the Holy Spirit controls our lives
He will produce this kind of fruit in us:
love, joy, peace, patience, kindness, goodness, faithfulness, gentleness,
and self-control."
Galatians 5:22-23

And in the next verse, the Bible tells us what love is:

"Love is patient, love is kind. It does not envy, it does not boast,
it is not proud. It does not dishonor others, it is not self-seeking,
it is not easily angered, it keeps no record of wrongs. Love does not
delight in evil but rejoices with the truth. It always protects,
always believes, always hopes, always perseveres.
Love never fails…"
1 Corinthians 13:4-8

The characteristics described in those two scriptures are the characteristics you will see in a godly person and in a real Christian.

I hope every Christian reading this will be sure to examine ourselves and our own behavior. It's the adversary who pretends to be a Christian with the distinct objective to turn people away from God.

Having said that, if you are a believer and wondering why life still sucks, this could be why. Examine if your behavior aligns with what God calls His children to do and be. The Holy Spirit dwelling within us is what makes the difference *(Galatians 5:16-25). 1 John Chapter 3*, among many, is another magnificent place to find more clarity in this area.

Number 2
"Heart Disease"
Believing With an Unclean Heart

This is one of the biggest reasons many people don't experience the promises of God or see true change in their lives, but it can surely be resolved with the proper insight and steps, which we are about to discuss.

It's easy for someone to fool people into believing whatever they want them to, if they're a good actor; however, God cannot be tricked. Many people think that *acting* the part means that they *are* the part. This is far from the truth. God knows our innermost thoughts, motives, and desires. If we're going to truly serve, love, and honor God, the first step (after accepting Jesus as our Lord and Savior) is understanding that true change comes from within, from our hearts. The heart is the core; the thing that must be given to God first and foremost for Him to cleanse.

"The heart is deceitful above all things, and desperately wicked: who can know it? Only the Lord knows! He searches all the hearts and examines deepest motives so he can give to each person his right reward, according to his deeds—how he has lived."
Jeremiah 17:9-10

"Above all else, guard your heart, for everything you do flows from it."
Proverbs 4:23 NIV

The NLT version says:

"Guard your heart above all else,
for it determines the course of your life. "
Proverbs 4:23 NLT

We learned in Chapter 8 that the heart, in its natural and fleshly state, is in conflict with the things of God (the Spirit). When we give our lives, minds, bodies, and souls to God, we begin to operate and be led by the Spirit instead of the flesh.

It's pivotal for humans to understand that the course and quality of our lives is determined by the condition of our hearts.

Therefore, we must ask God to examine our hearts and re- move anything unclean *(Psalms 139:23-24)*. It's normal to have an unclean heart when you come to Jesus *(Matthew 11:28-30)*. God has a way of revealing His existence and power by changing you and helping you do things only possible through His power.

When you choose God, it can't just be because you want peo- ple to love you or because you want to be admired and blessed. There cannot be any selfish desires behind your faith in God. You must honor and obey God because He is God, because He loves you, and because you love Him, not because you want to excel and be great. We know this comes with the territory of having pure and genuine faith. We know prosperity is a result of surren- dering your life to God *(1 Kings 2:3, Psalms 1:2-3)* because God makes this clear all throughout the Bible; however, this can't be the sole reason you're doing it. Your ultimate *why* must be because you want to glorify God and help others see His greatness through you. This desire is something that emerges as you develop a personal relationship with the Lord—spending time with Him, getting to know Him, and growing closer to Him.

Often, people will turn to God, change, and walk with Him during a crisis, but as soon as they get what they want, or as soon as the smoke clears, they say, "OK God, I'm good now. I'll take it from here!" Then, they make the mistake of reverting back to their old ways. Some people become blessed and conveniently forget that God got them where they are, and they stop giving Him credit as if they got themselves there.

God knows our hearts. He knows things about us that we don't even know. He knows what we will and won't do, and He rewards us accordingly. So what's important, first and foremost, is sincerely asking God to cleanse your heart and genuinely having a clean heart. This is when the promises of God will begin to manifest in your life.

Everything we do has to be about glorifying God, not about personal gain. As your faith grows, God will change your heart and cause it to want the things that it should *(Psalms 37:4)*. He gives you desires that prosper you and that have a positive impact on everyone around you.

So ask yourself these questions:

1. Am I going to God because there is something I want, and once I get it, will I go back to life as usual?
2. Am I going to God because I want to be praised and liked by people?
3. Am I going to God primarily for personal or financial gain?

If you answered yes to these questions, you may very well have the wrong motives and desires. They won't ignite the type of favor that you truly desire and expect.

Here is a great key that worked for me: When I made a decision to give my life to the Lord, I wanted to make sure I was in it wholeheartedly and in it for life. Therefore, I imagined the worst thing that could happen to me, and I asked myself, *"Will you still love God?"* This is so key. The interesting thing is, I wasn't sure at first. I was thinking, *"Oh man, this would be hard."* But I kept imagining it and picturing myself trusting God through it. This solidified my faith.

This type of forward thinking helps me feel solid and secure in my faith, and it keeps me from the impediment of being unpleasantly surprised. It helps and leads me to *know,* beforehand, that I will love and trust God through even the deepest of trials. This is what it looks like to put God first and foremost, unconditionally. It's a real relationship. As humans, we give this place to other human beings, although it's God who should have first place in our hearts.

Remember to be sure your pursuance and affection for God is *not* all about *you.*

Before I came to Christ, I finally realized that what I wanted wasn't good for me, so I stopped caring about doing what I wanted. My life became about what God wants for me, not about what I want for myself. Now, of course, I want the best in life. Who doesn't? However, I was able to understand that the best comes when we genuinely love and honor God with all our heart, mind, and soul—His number one commandment. If you want God's favor upon you, your life, and everything you do, start with

pursuing and having a clean heart. Pursue it, acquire it, and protect it.

"Create in me a clean heart, O God;
and renew a right spirit within me."
Psalms 51:10 KJV

Number 3
Thinking That Believing Is All It Takes

This section piggybacks off of a subject we just touched on in the
previous chapter, but it goes a little more in detail with specific
scripture to back it up. As mentioned, a common mistake that
many believers make is thinking that believing is all it takes to be
a Christian and to live a better life. However, there is more to
being a Christian and a true child of God because, remember, even
demons believe and know God is real and all-powerful *(James
2:19)*. The following magnificent and important Bible passage
tells us exactly what it takes to live a better life and what it takes
to inherit the promises of God. (Note: I included the verse numbers in case you're comparing and reading from a different
translation. Also, I added numbering where the scripture lists key
required components.)

2 Peter 1:2-11 TLB
"Do you want more and more of God's kindness and peace? Then
learn how to know him better and better. (3) For as you know him
better, he will give you, through his great power, everything you need
for living a truly good life: he even shares his own glory and his own
goodness with us! (4) And by that same mighty power he has given us

all the other rich and wonderful blessings he promised; for instance,
the promise to save us from the lust and rottenness all around us,
and to give us his own character.

*(5) **BUT TO OBTAIN THESE GIFTS, YOU NEED MORE***
THAN FAITH;
[1] You must also work hard to be good,
and even that is not enough. For then
[2] You must learn to know God better and
discover what he wants you to do. Next,
[3] Learn to put aside your own desires so that you will become
patient and godly, gladly letting God have his way with you.
This will make possible the next step…
[4] Which is for you to enjoy other people and to like them,
and finally you will grow to love them deeply.
[Verse 8] The more you go on this way, the more you will grow
strong spiritually and become fruitful and useful to our Lord Jesus
*Christ. (9) **But anyone who fails to go after these additions to***
***faith** is blind indeed, or at least very shortsighted, and*
has forgotten that God delivered him from the old life of sin
so that now he can live a strong, good life for the Lord.
*(10) So, dear brothers, **work hard to prove that you really are***
among those God has called and chosen, and then you will
***never stumble or fall away.** (11) And God will open wide*
the gates of heaven for you to enter into the eternal kingdom
of our Lord and Savior Jesus Christ."

It took me a while to unravel the confusion surrounding whether we are saved by faith alone or faith *and* works, which we just covered in Chapter 11. If you happen to still be confused in any way about this, don't worry. I was too at first. Keep learning. God will bring clarity to you in due time. In the meantime, I'll say this: God's stance on obedience is clear. So, we have two options: We can either take God's *full* Word seriously, or we can ignore 98 percent of what it says. Don't do what the masses do and focus on that "one" confusing topic. When it comes to pleasing God and what God expects of us, the answer is crystal clear and written all over the Bible. We must focus on that. We know we are saved by faith, yes; however, we can't afford to ignore everything else Jesus says and neglect to connect the dots.

The New Testament is all about faith, works, and love. Meditate on what you *know* it says, not what you *don't* know it says, and you will be better off. Trust the guidance of the Holy Spirit. Ask Him to lead you and to reveal the truth. Don't focus too much on something that's confusing you because there's far more to focus on that isn't confusing. Keep learning and growing in love and in Christ, and it will all come together!

Number 4
Having One Foot in and One Foot Out

The majority of problems that people face are a direct result of fornication, idolization, lying, adultery, and many other sins— most of which have been completely normalized in society today. *This* is why we are experiencing more and more dysfunction in the world.

Idolatry—relying on people's approval, materialistic possessions, and human relationships to fulfill our lives instead of God—can easily invoke the wrath of God. This is evident all throughout the Bible, especially the Old Testament, where God clearly displays His discontent with idolization and putting other gods and things before Him.

Believers in this category "love and honor God" or *say* they do, but as we learned in the previous chapter, Jesus makes it clear in *John 14:15* what "loving God" looks like to God:

> *"'If you love me, you will keep my commandments.'"*
> *John 14:15 ESV*

> *"But those who keep on sinning are against God, for every sin is done against the will of God. And you know that he became a man so that he could take away our sins, and that there is no sin in him. So if we stay close to him, obedient to him, we won't be sinning either; but as for those who keep on sinning, they should realize this:* ***They sin because they have never really <u>known him</u> or become his."***
> *1 John 3:4-6 NLT*

So, if you're a believer who's trying to figure out why what you've been doing isn't working, examine if you have made a practice of sinning and thinking that these actions have no effect on the quality of your life. They do, indubitably.

Number 5
Believing in God but Not Jesus

Some people believe in God, the Creator, but refuse to believe in Jesus. Here is one scripture from the good book that tells us about the significance of believing in the Son of God, Jesus:

"...And God declares that Jesus is his Son. All who believe this know
in their hearts that this is true. If anyone doesn't believe this,
he is actually calling God a liar,
because he doesn't believe what God has said about his Son.
And what is it that God has said? That he has given us eternal life,
and that this life is in his Son. So whoever has God's Son has life;
whoever does not have his Son, does not have life.
I have written this to you who believe in the Son of God so that you
may know you have eternal life. And we are sure of this, that he will
listen to us whenever we ask him for anything in line with his will.
And if we really know he is listening, when we talk to him and
make our requests, then we can be sure that he will answer us."
1 John 5:9-15 TLB

As proven in God's Word, belief in Jesus, the Son of God, is crucial for a believer.

"For a person who doesn't believe in Christ, God's Son,
can't have God the Father either. But he who has Christ,
God's Son, has God the Father also."
1 John 2:23 TLB

Number 6
Fully Trusting God but Partly Trusting His Word (the Bible)

I've noticed that people like to pick and choose which sections of the Bible they will believe and live by. If a person doesn't like something the Bible says, it isn't convenient for their way of life, or they feel there is nothing wrong with something they want to do, they justify their behavior by disregarding or twisting the words of the Bible to fit their needs. But how can two walk together if they don't agree *(Amos 3:3)*?

Most fail to realize that we can't pick and choose which parts we want to obey, believe, and apply to fit what's convenient for us. Many make this mistake and it's the reason life still sucks for them. How can *you* determine which parts are from God and which aren't, based on your own understanding and reasoning *(Isaiah 55:8-9, Proverbs 3:5-7)*?

Loving God means obeying and trusting His Word always, not just when it's convenient for us. I've heard people say we shouldn't trust the Bible because it was written by man. Well, if we can't trust the Bible, what can we trust? If the Word of God is not trustworthy, no other book in existence is. Those were written by man as well. We talk more about this in the next chapter. If we say we can't trust the Bible because man wrote it and then say God's Word is the truth, well then, which is it? If you call God's Word the truth then doubt what it says, are you doubting the truth?

We've discussed that we receive what we believe. I once heard someone say, "A person can find proof for anything they *choose* to believe." But, remember, there is only one truth. Be careful not to get sucked into the trap of only believing what God says when it's convenient for your way of living.

The Bible is God's way of speaking to us. I don't believe God would allow His Word to be twisted so much that we wouldn't know what to do and how to act in order to please Him and receive His promises. This is another reason that having a close and personal relationship with God is important. When we have a relationship and connection with Him, we are able to discern truth from lies. God puts the truth in our hearts and gives us the ability to truly know right from wrong *(Romans 1:19)*.

I always say a prayer for God to help me receive His Word in the way that *He* intended, and I pray that He will NOT allow me to misinterpret His Word. I'd rather have God pardon me as He deals with those who *allegedly* twisted His Word in the writing of the Bible than to be one who is not fit for the Kingdom due to not believing what God has proclaimed to be His Word.

If there's anything that I don't understand in the Bible, I ask God to help me understand and to reveal the truth to me so that I can live a life that is pleasing to Him. I say that and then I worry no more, trusting the Holy Spirit to guide me along the right path. As mentioned before, God knows our hearts. He knows if we are truly misinformed or if we are just doing what *we* want to do.

Number 7
Loving God but Not People

Anything God commands and advises us to do falls under the categories of loving Him, loving ourselves, and loving others.

> *"… Whoever is living a life of sin and doesn't love his brother shows that he is not in God's family; for the message to us from the beginning has been that we should love one another."*
> *1 John 3:10-11 TLB*

"Dear friends, let us practice loving each other, for love comes from
God and those who are loving and kind show that they are the
children of God, and that they are getting to <u>know</u> him better.
But if a person isn't loving and kind,
it shows that he doesn't <u>know</u> God—for God is love."
1 John 4:7-8 TLB

"If anyone says "I love God," but keeps on hating his brother,
he is a liar; for if he doesn't love his brother who is right there in
front of him, how can he love God whom he has never seen?
And God himself has said that one must love not only God,
but his brother too."
1 John 4:20-21 TLB

As you can see, there are many scriptures throughout *1 John* and other books of the Bible about the importance of loving others as God commands.

The Bible reminds us in *Luke 6:32-35* that it's easy to love those who love us, even sinners do that, but what about those who hate us? God commands us to love even our enemies. Yikes right? It isn't always easy to love others if they happen to be cruel to us, or just outright rude, mean, and inconsiderate. Trust me, I know. It isn't easy, by far. However, I've realized that it's a major upgrade in life, a special superpower, and a gift from God when we are able to love others and remain kind regardless of what others choose to do. This doesn't mean taking crap from anyone. It just means not holding resentment or hate in your heart towards anyone. Some people are extremely toxic with no true desire to get better. These are the types we should pray for and love from a distance. Loving others doesn't mean subjecting and joining yourself to toxicity.

God's commandments literally tell us how to love Him, ourselves, and others. His entire Word clearly tells us what love means and what it looks like. Wouldn't you want your children to love one another instead of fighting and hurting each other? God is no different when it comes to us, His children. He wants us to love one another.

We've discussed the *true* definition of love and the correct way to love others, not the world's dysfunctional depiction of love.

Number 8
You Are Too Nice

I decided to include this section because I'm guessing there are some Christians, somewhere in the world, who are miserable because they are too nice! They give and give and give selflessly and are often taken advantage of. They may give so much that, at times, they're completely depleted with nothing left to give themselves.

Though this is the epitome of kindness, we have to remember that we must know how to love ourselves before we can truly and adequately love someone else. Let's talk about self-love for a moment. Loving and obeying God is the prerequisite for self-love, because if you are *first* loving God, then you are obeying Him, and if you are obeying Him—then, inherently, you have no behaviors that would subject yourself to harm. When you truly love yourself, you don't initiate your own demise through self-sabotage and self-destructive behaviors. If you have God, you have wisdom, and with wisdom comes immaculate decision making.

Now, back to the topic at hand—being too nice. Wisdom comes from God, and wisdom is far from naive. There's wise and there's naive. They are two different things. Jesus was nice and loving. He wasn't naive. He wasn't tricked and deceived. He was nice because He wanted to be, not because He was manipulated and tricked. Be careful of this.

Loving God doesn't mean allowing people to walk all over you! It means helping those in need, praying for them, and not harboring feelings of bitterness or hatred toward anyone. It doesn't mean being naive. You can always help people from a distance. You must have healthy boundaries, discernment, and wisdom so the enemy doesn't draw you into hate and bitterness from others using and abusing you.

The devil will send people into your life for the sole purpose of stealing your joy, your energy, your sanity, your time, and the like. He comes to steal, kill, and destroy; so pay close attention to what's happening around you. Pray for discernment and separate yourself from leeches who only take and take. They drain all that you could be giving to someone who is truly in need, and they distract you from the people or things that God has actually called you to.

Remember, when you walk closely with the Lord, praying and reading His Word, He will give you wisdom and discernment. All you have to do is ask and trust Him to direct your path. As a Christian, it's important to know God's Word, which reveals the tricks of the devil; this way you will know them when you see them!

Number 9
Being a Hearer of the Word but Not a Doer

"But be doers of the word, and not hearers only,
deceiving yourselves."
James 1:22 NKJV

This is the biggest area that keeps people from experiencing change. Every other section we've discussed in this chapter boils down to this one. There are many people, sometimes even the most evil ones, who can tell you everything the Bible says, but they don't live by it or even believe in it. Some people are mistaken into believing that as long as they read it or hear it, they are saved. Not so.

The Word of God only works if you apply it. *This* is the game changer. The activator. The Word of God is the remedy, the answer, and the medicine, but you have to use it, not just hear it. How can someone go to church every Wednesday and Sunday yet be ungodly? Because they are hearers only.

Some say knowledge is power, but knowledge is useless if it isn't utilized. Many people have knowledge, but they don't apply it. For example, people know that drugs are harmful, that lying gets you nowhere in the long run, that smoking can kill you, that drinking or texting and driving is dangerous and can lead to death or injury, that committing adultery and any other sin will reap bad results in their lives—yet many will still engage in these unfruitful acts. Wisdom is having knowledge and actually applying it. Wisdom is not only knowing what's right, but doing it.

The best way to habitually and naturally apply wisdom is to agree with it. How can two walk together unless they agree *(Amos 3:3)?* If you agree that something is bad for you or bad in general, why not turn away from it? This is called *repenting.* If you can agree that lying, cheating, stealing, adultery, and so forth are not good, then walking with God will be much easier. If you don't agree with God and what He stands for, it won't be easy to walk with Him or stay with Him. So the important thing is to make sure that your views match God's views and that your desires match God's desires. At this point, you'll be walking in step. Now you'll be on your way to developing a real connection, bond, and relationship with the Lord. Now everything will begin to align, come together, and make sense. Now you'll begin to experience change, improvement, a new you, and a new life.

In closing this chapter, I want you to know that you are special, and you are loved. This chapter was solely designed to help anyone who may have been wondering why life can *still* be hard as a Christian and what you can do to turn things around!

Being a good person isn't about being perfect; it's about love and what's truly hidden deep within our hearts. Integrity is doing the right thing, even when no one's looking. That's what we should always strive for. As long as we continually look to God and look within ourselves, examining how we can grow in love, we're on the right track.

End-of-Chapter Reflection

Chapter 12
Why Life *Still* Sucks for Some Believers

1. Name three issues that could cause life to suck for a believer.

_____

_____

_____

_____

_____

_____

2. Of the nine reasons discussed, what is the *biggest* issue that keeps people from experiencing change? (*Hint: Answer is in the first sentence of the correct section.*)

_____

_____

_____

_____

_____

_____

3. How will you incorporate what you learned from Chapter 12 into your life today (and moving forward)?

_____

_____

_____

_____

_____

_____

_____

4. Name something new that you discovered about yourself (if applicable).

_____

_____

_____

_____

_____

_____

_____

5. Name something new or interesting that you learned about
God, life, and/or people.

_____

_____

_____

_____

_____

_____

_____

6. Journal any other notes, takeaways, or reminders that you'd like
to capture from Chapter 12.

_____

_____

_____

_____

_____

_____

_____

_____

Chapter 13

Apologetics
Most Asked Questions
and Answers About God

O ne day, my son told me he was asked the question, "Why would you believe in God if you've never seen Him?" and "Why would you believe in the Bible, considering man wrote it?" At first, I was a bit upset. This was someone we knew. Therefore, my first inclination was to confront this spiritually dead grown person for attempting to turn my child away from God and open my child up to the meaningless world of confusion and darkness that he himself was living in.

However, I suddenly remembered God's Word, "Be slow to anger." Then, the Holy Spirit impressed upon me that an even better response would be to use this as a teachable moment. There are people in the world—more now than ever—who question and discard the existence and credibility of God on a wide-scale basis. For that very reason, I began to see how this dilemma was actually

a good thing, because it allowed me to better prepare my kids for
the world before they are older and away from home. This way,
they won't be surprised, swayed, or thrown by the opinions of
others. In other words, these types of remarks and concepts won't
be anything new for them. I began to feel extremely blessed to
have the opportunity to prepare them for such a time as this.

The Bible tells us in *1 Peter 3:15 TLB:*

> *"Trust yourself to Christ your Lord and if anybody asks
> why you believe as you do, be ready to tell him,
> and do it in a gentle and respectful way."*

That being so, in compliance with the Holy Spirit and out of
curiosity, I asked my son, "So…what was your response?"

"Well, then…who made us?" he replied.

This response put a huge smile on my face.

And that, ladies and gentlemen, is what you call apologetics.
He responded with a rhetorical question, and not like a deer in
headlights; which, for a child, I thought was fantastic! He wasn't
thrown off. He made it clear to that person that their way of thinking made just as little sense to him as his way of thinking made to
them.

Dictionary.com defines apologetics as, "the branch of theol-
ogy concerned with the defense or proof of Christianity using
rational argument."

As you can see in *1 Peter 3:15,* God calls us to be ready to
provide reasoning for our faith, and to do it respectfully and gen-
tly. What an awesome God. I love that He gives us direction in

every way in life and tells us how to handle the situations we will face.

I wanted to include this chapter in case you have any questions about God and to help prepare you when you're approached by someone who has questions about your faith. In this chapter, I'm going to address the following most commonly asked questions:

1. Who made God?
2. Why do you believe in God if you've never seen Him?
3. Why believe in the Bible if man wrote it?
4. Why does God allow evil and suffering?
5. Why do bad things happen to good people?
6. How do we know which religion is true when there are so many?
7. How come we don't see God and miracles today like people used to?
8. The white man created Christianity and the Bible justifies slavery, why would you believe in such a thing?

Question 1
Who made God?

When we tell an unbeliever that God made us, they like to respond with, "Well, who made God?" The answer to this question is short and sweet.

No one made God. God is not made. He has always existed, and He has been here since the beginning of time. There is only one Creator, and He wasn't created. That's what makes Him God.

God was, is, and always will be *(Revelation 1:8, Revelation 21:6, Revelation 1:17).*

"'I am the Alpha and the Omega,
the Beginning and the End, the First and the Last.'"
Revelation 22:13 NKJV

This is really a dead end question, it will never go anywhere. No matter who or what someone believes is the creator, someone can or will always respond with, "Well, who created that?" For example, someone might believe that science created the world, but who created science? Did it create itself? If science can create itself, then God can too. You see?

Therefore, again, it's all about where you decide to get your answers from. I go to the Source. If God says He is the first, then that's what I believe. It makes sense to me. There's nothing He can't do. Why? Because He's God.

Question 2
Why do you believe in God if you've never seen Him?

"If all you see is what you see
then you do not see all there is to be seen."
- Dr. Tony Evans

Any question that challenges the existence of God falls under this category. I wanted to start here because my son provided a pretty good answer when his faith was challenged.

Who made us? Notice, my son didn't ask, "what" made us, he asked "who." My son was only ten years old at the time, but he was able to comprehend that we were created by someone, not something.

If you look at the world we live in, it's quite obvious it was created and designed by a being who has infinite intellect and power *(Romans 1:20)*. Look at the sun, the moon, the stars—I mean, I can really go on forever but, the sun! Come on. If we really think about it, who made it and holds it in place? The sun is *so* bright we can't even stare directly into it. Furthermore, it will burn our skin if we're exposed to it for too long, sometimes for only minutes. Imagine if the sun happened to get juuuuust a little too close. Actually, I don't want to imagine that! However, I can see that the *One* who is perfect and in control made sure that never happened.

Studies show that the world is covered with more than 70 percent water. Who keeps the ocean from completely overtaking and flooding the earth? Who created and ordered the seas to stay in place? The Bible answers this in *Proverbs 8:27-29*.

Not only that, but consider human beings. God made us in His image *(Genesis 1:26-27)*, so we are intellectual beings. We can think and feel. How could some"thing" or even no"thing" have created us? Furthermore, there are billions of human beings in existence, yet no two people have the same fingerprint. This is an identifying mechanism from your Creator. God knows the number of hairs on your head *(Luke 12:7)*. If God gave each of us our very own fingerprints, this proves we were particularly and specially made. How is all of this something that just happened from a nothingful, happenstance, meaningless big bang? I personally don't see how that is reasonable. It sounds to me like someone who will go to any stretch before they will acknowledge there is a God. The Bible tells us that at creation God said, "Let there be light." Maybe this is the bang they are referring to:

> *"Now the earth was formless and empty, darkness was over the surface of the deep, and the Spirit of God was hovering over the waters. And God said, 'Let there be light,' and there was light."*
> *Genesis 1:2-3 NIV*

Again, God created us in His own image; therefore, we have the capacity to think. We have intellect. We can make cars, ships, telephones, cell phones, computers, internet, WiFi, planes, electricity, and so forth. If mere humans, not being of infinite wisdom and power, can make all of these amazing things, how much more can God do?

I'm astounded by what human beings have created, but with all of humanity's inventions and creations, man can never create or invent what God has.

There are many things in the world that we cannot see, but we know they are real. Carbon monoxide (CO) is an odorless, colorless, toxic, and flammable gas. It's unsafe to leave a gas-powered vehicle running in a closed garage because carbon monoxide will build up and will lead to illness or death by poisoning. We cannot see carbon monoxide. Even when it's right in front of us and at a level so great it could kill us, we don't see it.

There are some things in life that don't have a physical form; you only know it's real because of the effect it has on people and things. We can't see good spirits or bad spirits, but we can see the effects they have on people and their lives. Thankfully, we decide which spirit we allow to dominate our lives.

If we step inside of a sauna, we can't see heat, but we can feel it. That's how we know it exists. We cannot see loneliness, but we can feel it. We can simply walk outside and look up in the sky or look around at all of the things man *didn't* create and know God exists. We don't have to see Him to know He's there *(2 Corinthians 4:18)*. God is love, and there's nothing greater than love. We know an act of God when we see or feel one. There are things in the world that cannot be explained by scientists. The inexplicable. The wonders of the world. Miracles. That's God.

Sometimes, we find beauty in nature that takes our breath away. That's God.

What about that sixth sense we get, known as our intuition or gut feeling? It lets us know something is wrong even though we may not *see* anything wrong. It's an innate sense that protects us, speaks to us, and guides us. That's God.

Every day, we experience and witness things that the Bible speaks of. Everything is as He says it is or will be. A book inspired by God and written thousands of years ago, the Bible, still holds true to its word today. That's God.

It's obvious that the words in the Bible are wisdom. If man actually listened and applied everything Jesus says, man would reach heights that he never imagined he could. That's because we have access to the power of God as heirs, if we so choose, called the Holy Spirit. It's a free gift from God for those who choose Him in faith and love. Most just never bother.

The answers I've provided may not be enough for some people, but it's enough for me. Just make sure that your answers are enough for you because they won't be enough for everyone. There are some who believe and some who don't. That isn't going to change until the day we meet our Maker; and when that time comes, only one side of the coin will lose. Because even if believers are wrong, we only believed in God and His Son Jesus and made good choices, which only bettered our lives. So, we can't lose. Those who *only* believe in what they can physically see will have to cross their fingers and hope they're right.

I recommend a movie called *God's Not Dead*, which currently has four parts. This movie series is excellent for anyone who has questions about God or wants to know how to answer questions about God.

"You love Him even though you have never seen Him.
Though you do not see Him now, you trust Him;
and you rejoice with a glorious, inexpressible joy.
The reward for trusting Him will be the salvation of your souls."
1 Peter 1:8-9 NLT

"Only fools say in their hearts, 'There is no God.' They are corrupt,
and their actions are evil; not one of them does good!"
Psalms 14:1 NLT

"For ever since the creation of the world
His invisible attributes, His eternal power and divine nature,
have been clearly seen,
being understood through His workmanship
[all His creation, the wonderful things that He has made],
so that they [who fail to believe and trust in Him]
are without excuse and without defense."
Romans 1:20 AMP

Question 3
Why believe the Bible if man wrote it?

The following verse is among the last words written in the closing of the Bible.

"And I solemnly declare to everyone who hears the words of prophecy written in this book: If anyone adds anything to what is written here, God will add to that person the plagues described in this book. And if anyone subtracts any part of these prophecies, God shall take away his share in the Tree of Life, and in the Holy City just described."
The Revelation 22:18-19

Considering the Bible is God's most prominent way of communicating with us and leading us to faith and the knowledge of who He is, I don't believe that God would allow the Bible to be corrupted.

If the Bible truly was corrupted, we would be left with no idea of who God is and what He wants from us and for us. That's number one. Number two, how did writing the Bible benefit the men who wrote it? Think about it. Many of these people were killed back then just for speaking up for God, Jesus, and righteousness. How did they benefit from making up anything in the Bible?

All the Bible consists of are events that people witnessed in the world and wrote about. We as human beings have been doing this from the beginning of time. If we can't believe in the occurrences or history of the Bible because man wrote it, that means we can't believe *anything* ever written by man because man wrote every book. Can you see how this notion simply holds no weight?

The only reason we know about anything that happened in history is because people who lived during that time wrote about it. That's what humans do. My mother was alive when MLK was alive. His life was documented by men. She was watching the television and saw how devastated her parents and everyone around her were when the news broke of his assassination.

Events like this can be written and sustained throughout history because there were people alive when it happened. *The Titanic* is another example. People who were alive back then wrote about what happened. Eyewitnesses are the only reason we have inside information.

I lived during the coronavirus pandemic, and I lost someone very dear to me. I saw what the virus did to him. I saw how it literally took his breath away and finally, took his life away. This was a big, strong, healthy man, as far as we all knew. Gerald Simmons, who was like a father to me. I called him dad. He was my dad.

I was alive during the Hurricane Katrina catastrophe. I was a few miles from New York City, stationed at McGuire AFB, New Jersey, watching the news when two hijacked airplanes deliberately crashed into the World Trade Center buildings. Millions of people witnessed these events, same as many other major events throughout history.

If it makes it to the status of "history," something everyone in the world has heard of, normally it was *witnessed* by a substantial number of people. I don't benefit from telling you I was alive when these catastrophes occurred. I don't benefit from telling you

what I witnessed. Same as the people who witnessed and documented everything written in the Bible.

These events wouldn't still be talked about today if there were
no witnesses, truth, or validity to the occurrence of the events recorded. I say again, if you can't trust the Bible, you can't trust
anything written over 300 years ago because much of it is substan-
tiated by eyewitness accounts.

God did something to show us He is real. He made sure we
knew who He was and how the world and everything in it came
to be. He revealed His existence to the world so that it could be
recorded; meanwhile, telling us all we need to know about Him
and the purpose of life in order for us to make a free will decision
before He comes back. He made it clear He will be here in Spirit
for now, but He *will* be back, and everyone will stand before Him
on judgment day and answer for everything they did or didn't do
while living on Earth. Every knee *will* bow before Jesus *(Romans
14:10-12)*.

God doesn't overtly show Himself today like He did in Bible
days. This reminds me of those movies where a person is rich or
royal, but they don't want people to cling to them just because of
their status. So, they don't tell anyone who they are, because they
want to see who will choose them regardless. They want to see
what truly lies within a person's heart.

That's how I feel about the way God moves today. He has
already made His existence and presence known. He provided us
with plenty of information, and He now has the opportunity to
see what each of us is really made of. As He populates His Kingdom, He will know that every person is there because, with their
own free will, they chose to be—because they love who He is and

what He stands for. They listened to Him, trusted Him, recognized Him, and welcomed Him in a world full of people who opposed Him.

That is who His Kingdom will be filled with one day, if you ask me. He will know who truly loves Him. He will be around people who decided to love and trust Him; and even though they've never seen Him, they *knew* Him. He will know who truly *wanted* to know Him and be close to Him. He will know who truly valued truth and love—and who devotedly sought to be better for God, themselves, and mankind.

I love the Lord with all my heart because He is everything this world is not. God speaks against all of the corruption and darkness in the world; what type of person would be against that? Just food for thought. I'd be happier to teach my kids about that great guy in the sky named God than I would be to teach them about Santa Claus. Santa can't help us. He brings gifts once a year to "kids who are good," parents say. However, God brings gifts—eternally—to those who seek Him.

My last point on this matter is this—God was in control when His Word was constructed. His Holy Spirit directed His chosen people in delivering His Word to us *(2 Timothy 3:16-17)*. If anyone believes that man is powerful enough to corrupt God's Word and leave us all confused with no concept of the truth, that means they don't believe He is God. That means they don't believe He is in control of even His own Word. That's more of a doubt in God's power, influence, and credibility than the men who wrote the Bible. In other words, you're not doubting man, you're doubting God.

In conclusion, if we can't believe in the Bible because man wrote it, we can't believe anything else written by man; not our history books or any other book.

If this is the case, we have nothing, and we can't learn anything from our ancestors, so why try? Burn all books, if that's good reasoning, because man wrote every single book on the planet. Humans are the only ones who *can* write books. If we were told that the Bible was written by angels or God Himself, the naysayers wouldn't believe that either. I said it once, I'll say it again—with some people, God can't win. They have a desire to doubt everything about God, and they always will. The Bible speaks of them. Read up! That way, when certain voices come your way, you'll know who sent them.

"For no prophecy recorded in Scripture was ever thought up by the prophet himself. It was the Holy Spirit within these godly men who gave them true messages from God."
2 Peter 1:20-21 TLB

The Bible was not just written by man. It was written by men who were alive and there when God revealed Himself to the world and made His existence known. It was documented, and it's up to man at this point to choose his beliefs and his fate. This tells God a lot when the time comes for Him to bring all of this to an end. You have free will, what will you do with it?

Question 4

Why does God allow evil and suffering?

When God created us, He gave us the free will to make our own decisions. If there is no good or bad, then do we really have a choice? If there is no good or bad, what are we choosing? If there was nothing but good, then there is no choice to make.

I believe God wants to see what YOU would choose, given the option. Even more, He wants *you* to know what *you* would choose. This way, there will be no excuse come Judgment Day.

God doesn't make decisions for people and God is not responsible for the behaviors of human beings; especially ones who aren't listening to Him. God's command for us is: *to love.* Why blame God for what humans choose to do with their own free will? So, to answer the question, there is evil in the world because that is what people *choose* to do. But God will always vindicate you if you are harmed by someone, as He promises in His Word. That is, when you obey Him. Things will eventually go south for evil-doers—but, if you take matters into your own hands or turn from God, the same applies to you—things will go south and they will keep going south. God detests evil even more than we do, and there is always a price to pay for turning away from the wisdom and righteousness of God—even if we think we have a good reason to. This is why it's never wise to allow the behavior of others to negatively impact your behavior and character.

"God will repay each person according to what they have done."
Romans 2:6 NIV

In the story of Noah and the Ark and throughout the Old Testament, God purged the land of evil on several occasions and had massive numbers of people wiped out because of their evil intentions, actions, and desires. Many people will call God cruel because of this, then in the same breath will ask why He won't stop evil.

When it comes to suffering, I can't tell you *why* we suffer, per se, but I can tell you we do not suffer in vain—not God's children. I believe those who oppose God suffer in vain, but that's their choice. I addressed the issue of pain and suffering in Chapter 10, so be sure to take another look at that if you need help wrapping your mind around this particular aspect of life.

Question 5
Why do bad things happen to good people?

Bad things seem bad to us because we don't understand God, His purpose, and His power. God has the ability to take us through something unpleasant and have it turn out to be the best thing that ever happened to us. If something bad happens to a good person—a truly good person—there is a reason beyond what you can see.

In an apologetics interview, I heard a powerful statement by Dr. Frank Turek in response to the question, "How can God murder in the Old Testament yet command us not to?" Dr. Turek's answer was that when people die they don't really die, they just change location. They go from this life into the next life, and it's up to God when that happens. In that case, can God murder anyone? No, because God is the Creator of life, the Sustainer of life, and He's the only one who can resurrect life. In this case, what might be immoral for us is not immoral for God. If that's the case then God murders all of us one day because we all die. It isn't murder when God decides to transition us from this life to the next. Talk about apologetics, wow! What a great response from Dr. Turek.

The sooner humans learn to trust God, the more sense things will make and the clearer the picture will become. I don't know anyone who trusted God through hard times and regretted it. We hear about this all the time throughout life and history—tragic experiences that ended up changing people's lives for the better. God always has a reason for anything that happens to us, and God's plans are always to prosper us. Our ways are not His ways and our thoughts are not His thoughts.

This concept is the hardest to comprehend, but the simple truth is, everything God does has a domino effect, and all things work together for the *good* of those who love the Lord. We have to trust His plan. When someone gives up during tough times, it doesn't usually get better, but things always turn around in unimaginable ways for those who keep their trust and faith in the Lord regardless of their circumstances. The following scripture proves God is aware of everything that is going on with us. He *is* in control.

"Many are the afflictions of the righteous,
but the LORD delivers him out of them ALL."
Psalms 34:19 KJV

This brings me back to a previous example. Jesus was not only good, He was perfect, but look at what happened to Him on Earth. Furthermore, think of MLK and Joseph from the book of Genesis. These were good men who suffered greatly; however, their afflictions did not defeat them but elevated them, the world, and their life's work.

> *"Even though Jesus was God's Son,*
> *he learned obedience from the things he suffered.*
> *In this way, God qualified him as a perfect High Priest,*
> *and he became the source of eternal salvation for all those who*
> *obey him."*
> *Hebrews 5:8-9 NLT*

It isn't about us. I can't say this enough. Anyone who gets upset about what happens to them individually doesn't understand that their reason for existence is bigger than just them. Everything we experience here is temporary. Just like it was for Jesus, Joseph, MLK, and others. We need to focus on successfully doing what we were sent here to do and going back home. We each have a cross to bear—a problem or problems to overcome—and God is with us through it all, if we so choose—and we will not lose.

> *"Yet what we suffer now is nothing compared to*
> *the glory He will give us later."*
> *Romans 8:18 TLB*

My best recommendation for anyone struggling with heartache and pain is for you to hear from people who have gone through the exact same turmoil as you, yet they overcame and came out on top of it. Talk to people who kept the faith through the storm. Learn about their experience, their outcome, and how they did it. There are success stories of all kinds after tribulation. The only stories that don't end well are the ones who gave up before they reached their glory—or never walked with God to begin with.

They say it's darkest just before dawn. Most throw in the towel before the sun rises.

"Many of life's failures are people who did not realize
how close they were to success when they gave up."
- Thomas A. Edison

This is why God urges us to not get weary in good works, to persevere through turmoil, and to never give up *(Galatians 6:9)*. Don't ever give up because, if so, you end up going through it all for nothing. Don't go through all of this for nothing.

Listening to genuine human testimony is the best way to understand. Like the story of the two brothers, there are people who go through the exact same trials, yet their lives and outcomes are totally different. Why is that? It's not what happened to them, but how they responded to it.

"Life is 10 percent what happens to you
and 90 percent how you react to it."
- Charles R. Swindoll

Question 6

How do we know which religion is true

when there are so many?

I'm not an expert on every religion; however, from the basic amount of research I've done, it seems to me that they all have the following in common: We are to love and honor God, and we are to love and respect one another. With that said, I think that's a great place to start and it validates what the Bible declares as the greatest command of all—*Love*.

When it comes to the Christian faith, I believe God represents the ultimate expression of love. He sacrificed His only Son, an extension of Himself, giving us a way to be made right with Him. Furthermore, He is merciful, graceful, and forgiving. He doesn't expect us to be perfect and to reach Him by checking boxes, but simply by faith working through love.

One distinguishable factor that stands out to me is that the Christian faith offers salvation. I'm not certain that any other religion guarantees salvation in this way.

In Christianity, God doesn't want to force us to do anything—rather, He wants us to love willingly and happily of our own free will. His Holy Spirit is what gives us the ability to live a life pleasing to the Lord, and the Holy Spirit is freely available to all who are open to receiving Him.

In this area of concern, pray to God and ask Him to lead you in the way that you should go. If you truly want to find truth, God will lead you to it. If you genuinely seek to please and know Him, He will be happy to lead you. If researching every religion is what you need to do in order to make a decision, then maybe that is what you should do. After evaluating them all, see which one calls to you, but make sure God is involved in this journey.

> *"Then you will call on me and come and pray to me,*
> *and I will listen to you. You will seek me and find me*
> *when you seek me with all your heart."*
> *Jeremiah 29:12 -13 NIV*

Question 7
How come we don't see God and miracles today like they used to?

Jesus advised His disciples that He would only be with them for a little while before He would leave and go back to be with the Father—but that He would return again someday *(John 16:16-22)*. The Bible tells us about the final coming of the Lord and how no one knows that day or time. Therefore, the Lord is doing exactly what He said He would. Jesus told His disciples to spread the word so we can be ready for His final return.

I believe God shows up in different ways today, similar to the examples used in question number two. When people have occurrences and doctors say they shouldn't have survived or won't ever recover but those people recover and are still here—those are miracles. There are times where we know divine intervention occurred, and I believe that's how God shows up today. The inexplicable—those "There's no way!" types of scenarios are where we know something divine took place.

Question 8
The white man created Christianity and the Bible justifies slavery. Why would you believe in such a thing?

I was speaking with someone one day. She was telling me about how empty and lost she felt in life. I asked her about her relationship with God. She told me she had questions about God. She expressed that she had heard people say the white man created Christianity and that the Bible condones slavery.

She was concerned about how horribly white people treated black people in history, during the time of slavery. Some people allege that the Bible justifies their behavior. However, this is far from the truth. White people couldn't have created the Bible and Christianity to justify their inhumane slavery practices because hate, maltreatment, and the oppression of people is the direct opposite of what the Bible and Christianity teaches. The Bible and Christianity did not justify the things they were doing.

Why would someone create and mass produce a book that contradicts everything they do? That just simply and literally wouldn't make any sense. It's important to test the information you hear by looking into it for yourself.

Joshua 9:3-26 entails the story of how one form of slavery came about, and in this particular case, it was a request, it wasn't forced upon them. In Bible times, people could request to work as a slave, or *servant*, in order to pay off their debts.

Here are a few Bible verses that reference slavery, or serving. These verses clearly state God and the Bible's stance on slavery. We will discuss more after viewing these scriptures.

*"And you slave owners **must** treat your slaves right, just as I have told them to treat you. Don't keep threatening them; remember, you yourselves are slaves to Christ; you have the same Master they do, and he has no favorites."*
Ephesians 6:9 TLB

If you only read *Ephesians 6:5-8*, which comes directly *before* the scripture we just read, it can easily be taken out of context. This is why you have to know the message surrounding the entire scripture, not just small pieces. *Ephesians 6:5-8* tells slaves to obey and serve their masters wholeheartedly. This verse can be misconstrued, if you stop there. In the next verse, *Ephesians 6:9*, which we just read (above), we can see that the Bible clearly tells slave owners to treat their slaves the exact same way—just, respectful, and lovingly. Conclusively, *Ephesians 6:5-9*, in its entirety, tells slaves to serve their masters well, but it *also* commands slave owners to do the exact same and treat their slaves right, just, and lovingly. The Bible commands the exact same thing of everyone, which it has commanded since the beginning of time: *love.*

Just because something happened in the Bible doesn't mean God condones it. Cain murdered Abel in the Bible out of jealousy, does that mean God condones that? Absolutely not.

"That evening as the sun was going down,
a deep sleep fell upon Abram,
and a vision of terrible foreboding, darkness, and horror.
Then Jehovah told Abram,
'Your descendants will be oppressed as slaves
in a foreign land for 400 years.

But <u>I will punish the nation that enslaves them,</u>
and at the end they will come away with great wealth.'"
Genesis 15:12-14 TLB

The book of Exodus goes into detail about God's people being enslaved and Him leading them out. I recommend reading the entire book of Exodus. Remember, be sure to read a version that's easier for you to understand. For me, it's The Living Bible (TLB). You can always read and compare different versions for an even deeper understanding.

"'If you buy a Hebrew slave, whether a man or a woman, you must
free him at the end of the 6th year you have owned him and don't
send him away empty handed. Give him a large farewell present
from your flock, your olive press, and your wine press.
Remember that you were slaves in the land of Egypt
and the Lord your God rescued you!'"
Deuteronomy 15:12-15 TLB

*"'If a slave escapes from his master, you **must not** force him to*
return; let him live among you in whatever town he shall choose,
*and **do not oppress him**.'"*
Deuteronomy 23:15-16 TLB

Conclusion

It's paramount to know the Bible for yourself in order to avoid being misinformed by the rationalizations, assumptions, and allegations of others.

If the white man created the Bible and Christianity, those who condoned or participated in the maltreatment of black people weren't following any of the rules inside of it when it came to slavery, oppression, hate crimes, and racism—which is the opposite of what the Bible stands for. I don't see how these biblical findings support that the white man created Christianity or that the Bible, God, or Christianity ever condoned malevolent slavery practices.

People have many questions when it comes to God. This is understandable. There's nothing wrong with asking or having questions—and researching for answers is a good thing. It helps you to know and understand why you believe as you do, it solidifies your faith, and it allows you to be prepared when the time comes for you to explain to someone why you believe as you do.

If you have more questions, I encourage you to go out and learn more about apologetics. I've found that there are people who have compiled a substantial amount of scientific and historical information that solidifies our faith. They do this for a living. Nowadays, with the internet and search engines—a lot of information, education, and videos are readily available at our fingertips. You should definitely look up apologetics and check it out!

End-of-Chapter Reflection

Chapter 13
Apologetics: Most Asked
Q&As About God

1. Of the eight areas covered, which Q&A section(s) resonated the most with you?

_____

_____

_____

_____

_____

_____

2. What are your biggest takeaways from Chapter 13?

_____

_____

_____

_____

_____

_____

_____

_____

3. How will you incorporate what you learned from Chapter 13 into your life today (and moving forward)?

_____

_____

_____

_____

_____

_____

_____

_____

4. Name something new that you discovered about yourself (if applicable).

_____

_____

_____

_____

_____

_____

_____

_____

5. Name something new or interesting that you learned about God, life, and/or people.

_____

_____

_____

_____

_____

_____

_____

_____

_____

_____

6. Journal any other notes, takeaways, or reminders that you'd like to capture from Chapter 13.

_____

_____

_____

_____

_____

_____

_____

_____

_____

_____

_____

_____

_____

_____

_____

_____

Chapter 14

Walking With God
Keys to Success

If this book has led you to an understanding and perception of God and faith that you've never had before, and if you would like to make the life-changing decision of accepting Jesus into your heart as Lord, Savior, and head of your life, congratulations! Wise CHOICE. Reverence for the Lord is the beginning of wisdom.

Every step you take with the Lord brings you closer and closer to living your best life and being your best self. You've begun the journey of focusing on what truly matters in life. Once you go all in and experience the goodness of God—His greatness, power, and love—you'll never want to return to your old dysfunctional way of living!

If you're ready and you haven't already received salvation by welcoming Jesus as your Lord and Savior, a prayer made especially for you can be found at the end of Chapter 8. Once you pray that prayer, you literally become a child of God, like Jesus. You become set apart. People should be able to know you are *not* from this world and that you belong to God by the way you think and act. Look to God in all you do, and allow Him to begin working on you. *"In all your ways acknowledge Him, and He shall direct your path" (Proverbs 3:6 NKJV).*

The best day of my life was the day I went all in with God, and it was the best decision I ever made. I believe it will be the same for you! We've already discussed the key aspects, components, and steps to transforming your life; so, in this final chapter, I wanted to share with you a few additional pointers, which will help you succeed along your way to becoming all God created you to be!

A Set Mindset

The first step and key is beginning your journey with the right mindset and expectations. It's important to understand that change is a process. It's awesome and amazing if you're able to 100 percent change overnight—but normally, change is a process, and you can expect to experience growing pains. Push through them. Just like a good old-fashioned workout! Let it burn! This is how you crucify your flesh and cause it to lose power over you! It's a good thing! Don't let this be a discouraging factor. Once your growing pains are over, you'll be reaching heights you never knew you could. It's well worth it.

During this time, don't beat yourself up if you happen to make a mistake. Keep practicing and keep looking to God, asking Him to help you overcome your flesh and any weaknesses. He will do it because this is in line with His will. This is the time where patience is developed. Patience is a virtue, a fruit of the Spirit, and a very important and necessary quality to have as a human being, child of God, and follower of Christ. If it seems like God isn't there or doesn't hear you, He does. Keep the faith, have patience, and you will be very surprised at where this takes you. Don't ever worry. Trusting God means we *know* He has everything under control—and we don't worry!

The following keys will help you avoid the common pitfalls that most humans fall into. You're not expected to be perfect; however, never *plan* to sin, but actively and intentionally *arrange* to avoid it. Meaning, don't put yourself in situations where you know it'll be difficult for you to do the right thing. Make a conscious effort to set yourself up for success by thinking ahead. Remember, continue to ask the Holy Spirit to help you. He will. You don't have to rely on your own strength! Do your part, and God will do His. Walk in wisdom. Obedience and transformation are a lot easier to master when we don't continually place ourselves in tempting situations. It's easier to avoid cookies and soda if there aren't any in the cabinet.

When it comes to mindset, it's important to have your mind made up in a non-wavering capacity. The enemy sturdily attempts to trip you up during this time because he does *not* want to see you win. He doesn't want you to get close to God and break free from the mental prison he's been holding you hostage in.

We learned that when you're walking with God, you're backed by the highest power, and you have authority over the enemy. So, there's nothing to fear when you face spiritual warfare.

"For God has not given us a spirit of fear,
but of power and of love and of a sound mind."
2 Timothy 1:7 NKJV

I want to make a very important distinction. I just mentioned that God has not given us the spirit of fear. However, the Bible says *fear* of the Lord is the beginning of wisdom. The word *fear* in this tense is not referring to being terrified. It means you recognize, respect, and acknowledge who He is—His power and His authority. It's the same type of fear that we would have for a loving parent. We know they have the power to, and will, punish us if we disobey. We recognize their power. We aren't terrified of our parents, because we know they love us and want the best for us. We know they correct us to keep us on the right path and to protect us, not to harm us. It's describing reverent fear.

Additionally, sometimes we use the word fear or afraid as a figure of speech. For example, we will sometimes say or hear things like this, "I'm *afraid* to tell you this, but your application has been denied." In this case, the person isn't literally afraid or in fear. What they mean in this tense of the word is "I care about you and your feelings, and it pains me to tell you this."

So, in the same way, having a reverent fear of the Lord means we care about Him. It means the relationship we have with Him is important to us. When we really love God, we won't *want* to do anything that will hurt or disappoint Him. It's no different when it comes to our other loved ones. When we have a true love for our spouse and other loved ones, we don't want to do anything that will hurt them. We love them so much that hurting them hurts us.

This is the same type of reverence we need to have for God, and this is the beginning of wisdom.

Now that we've established that, let's get back to our mindset. It's important to go into this with your mind made up. You have to make a decision that *this* is what you're doing and *nothing* is going to change that.

In the beginning, while you're an infant in this walk of faith, the devil will come at you with all types of temptation, because it's easier to destroy a baby than an adult. I'm using this as a metaphor. One day you will no longer be an infant in faith and the devil won't stand a chance. So, of course he will try to keep you from getting there.

It may suddenly seem like you just met the perfect person or perfect friend. Remember, we learned that the devil intentionally and often works through people to get to us, so you must be vigilant. Eyes open. I'm saying this because one thing I don't want to see happen is that you get discouraged and give up before you even begin. With that said, let's talk a little more about expectations.

It's important *not* to go into this journey thinking that everything will be perfect once you decide to follow God. Going all in with God doesn't mean every day and everything is going to be perfect. That isn't realistic; especially considering we are at war here. Will life be perfect? No. Will life be good? Yes, overall it will be. Will life be better? Absolutely.

Life will get better and better, but you have to stay the course when things don't look the way you think they should or when you feel like God doesn't hear you. He does. I've been there. He will always show up and give you confirmation that you're on the right path, as long as you stay positive and stay the course. Stick with God and let Him surprise you. After all, that's why today is called the present. You just never know what God will do from day to day. Keep growing stronger in your knowledge, wisdom, and faith in God, and you will be amazed. God literally tells us what to expect. All throughout the Bible, He lets us know, "If you do this, then I'll do that." So, if you really want to experience the promises of God and all He has for you, He tells you exactly how.

Be in the World but Not of It

Another key mindset factor in acquiring success along this journey is mentally and physically parting ways with the world. It'll be extremely hard to transform your life if you're still attached to and in love with the things and ways of the world.

"Do not conform to the pattern of this world, but be transformed by the renewing of your mind. Then you will be able to test and approve what God's will is—his good, pleasing, and perfect will."
Romans 12:2 NIV

It was much easier for me to make the transition because I got tired of the world and all it has to offer. This is the devil's world. God tells us this throughout the Bible—and, from experience, I know there's nothing to miss besides destruction and misery. This world hates God. I refuse to be a part of that.

At some point, it all became clear to me. Before my transformation, I did not have complete self-control. That was a major contributing factor to me realizing that this wasn't the type of life I wanted to live anymore—having no control over oneself—wanting to do right and knowing what's right, yet not having enough strength or control to do so—that wasn't living, that wasn't free-dom, and that wasn't happiness for me. Paul describes this very thing in *Romans 7:15-25*. This let me know that God understood exactly what I was going through, and that He was the answer.

You have to ask yourself, *do you really want a different life, or do you want to keep going through the same things you've been going through?* You can't have both—being led by the spirit *and* the flesh. That's called being double-minded or lukewarm, and that won't bring peace and happiness. There are many double-minded people in the world who operate in extreme dysfunction.

Choosing this walk means letting go of the empty and coun-terproductive desires and ways of the world and really beginning to experience a new life. A better life.

"Therefore if anyone is in Christ [that is, grafted in,
joined to Him by faith in Him as Savior]
he is a new creature [reborn and renewed by the Holy Spirit];
The old things [the previous moral and spiritual condition]
have passed away.
Behold, new things have come
[because spiritual awakening brings new life]."
2 Corinthians 5:17 AMP

"Those who belong to Christ Jesus have nailed the passions and
desires of their sinful nature to his cross and crucified them there.
Since we are living by the Spirit,
let us follow the Spirit's leading in <u>every</u> part of our lives."
Galatians 5:24-25 NLT

Keep God First

I hear people say these words all of the time without really doing so. As you begin this new lifestyle, it's imperative to make a decision to *literally* keep God first. Let's talk about what this means and what it looks like.

Keeping God first means: God above *all*. It means caring more about pleasing God than pleasing ourselves and other people. Keeping God first means—when I want to lie, I tell the truth instead. Keeping God first means—when I want to give up, I put my trust and faith in God to carry me to the finish line. It means walking away when I want to seek revenge. It means doing the right thing, no matter what everyone else does. Keeping God first means caring more about what God wants than what you want. It means caring more about what God says than what anyone else says. It means God is involved in *every* decision you make. *He* is the influencing factor in your life; the *only* One. If you are only listening to one voice—the voice of truth and love—you have stability and direction in the highest regard.

Another reason we should keep God first is because God is the one who encourages us to do better and be better every day. When we are better, our lives are better. When we are better, those around us are better.

It was vitally important for us to address the mindset aspect first and foremost because, as we learned, we must have the proper perspective and mindset in order to experience growth. Remember, change starts head first!

Now that we've discussed that, let's talk about where we go from here!

Establish Your Daily Routine

The number one thing we're working on is growing in faith. Faith comes by *hearing* the Word of God *(Romans 10:17)*; therefore, in order to grow in faith and really get to know the Lord, you *have* to read the Bible. Reading the Bible enables you to *know* and recognize the truth when you hear it and avoid being misled by inaccurate or false teachings. Accordingly, you must set out on a mission to read it *all*. It may seem impossible, but don't worry, it isn't at all. If you read some every day and focus on reading one entire Bible book at a time (Galatians, Romans, John, and so forth), you will eventually have read the whole thing before you know it. Take it day-by-day and step-by-step. One day, you will look up and realize you've read fifteen Books of the Bible, or even the entire New Testament. I recommend reading it—even just a little bit—every single day. If you would rather do Monday-Friday, Monday-Saturday, or something similar, that's better than once or twice a week. However, it's definitely time to make reading the Bible a part of your regularly scheduled program.

I make reading the Bible a part of my morning routine. Every morning when I wake up, I pray and talk to God. I thank Him for His blessings and I ask for Him to help me succeed at honoring Him and fulfilling His will.

If you would like a recommendation for prayer, I love a YouTube channel called *Grace for Purpose Prayers*. It's absolutely perfect for praying and teaching you the Word of God as well. Each video is usually about ten minutes long. They start out with a great lesson of the Word, and they continue with an awesome in-depth prayer. Be mindful that they have two similar channels:

Grace for Purpose and *Grace for Purpose <u>Prayers</u>*. One solely consists of a good Word, and one entails a good Word *and* prayer.

So, establish a daily routine for dedicating time to God. It's fine if you start with ten minutes every morning. As you grow closer to the Lord and build this new habit, you will likely end up dedicating more time as you go. It will likely become your favorite time of day, like a good workout or a cup of coffee. It will help you begin your day in the right way. Frequently spending time with God is what you were created to do—so, it will become very fulfilling and refreshing.

Remember to download my free PDF with "Where to Begin" instructions if you need help determining where to begin reading the Bible. We also discussed the importance of reading a Bible version that resonates best with you. As you know, I recommend my personal favorite, The Living Bible (TLB). NIV and NLT are also easier versions to understand, but there are many others for you to review and choose from.

Repetition is key, so don't hesitate to regularly revisit the chapters and information we've discussed in this book! Also, look into all resources, including book recommendations, that I've provided for you in the *Additional Resources* section. These will be extremely helpful as you embark upon this amazing and exciting new journey.

Helpful Tips

I'd like to share a few powerful tips which really helped me succeed in transforming my life.

I was fortunate to be in a place of isolation when I gave my life to Christ. This was beneficial because I didn't have a lot of distractions pulling me away and making it harder for me to stay the course.

I quickly learned that the things we watch, listen to, and expose ourselves to, all carry the possibility of influencing us in one way or another. It's important to watch and listen to things that *only* edify you. It's beneficial to stay away from music and movies that are filled with sex and other ideas that make you think in ways that could lead toward sinful desires and urges. The enemy works through the media, television, and music as well. If you're practicing celibacy, as unmarried believers should, it's advantageous to fast forward through sex scenes on TV. This makes such a big difference! Remember, thoughts lead to feelings, and feelings lead to actions. What we watch and listen to plants seeds in our minds. So, diminishing these influences makes it easier for us to focus on the right things—productive things that lead to a better life.

Thank you for reading my book! It has been my absolute pleasure spending this time with you and I look forward to doing it again soon! It is my sincere desire and hope that this experience has positively transformed your life in unimaginable ways!

As you well know, we are greatly influenced by the things people put out into the world, whether it's on a large-scale basis or in everyday life. We are *all* influencers, whether we want to be or not. Someone is watching you and being influenced by you, no matter who you are.

We have an impact on this world regardless of our status. Therefore, we have to ask ourselves the following questions: "When I speak and act, do my voice and actions influence people in a positive way or a negative way? Do my actions lead people out of darkness or into it? Do my actions lead people to love themselves and others, or do they encourage and perpetuate the cycle of toxicity, disobedience, and self-destruction?"

"But if you cause one of these little ones—those who believe in me— to stumble, it would be better for you to have a large millstone tied around your neck… What sorrow awaits the world, because it tempts people to sin. Temptations are inevitable, but what sorrow awaits the person who does the tempting.'"
Matthew 18:6-7

This may be an uncomfortable element to face, but it must be done. Stepping outside of your comfort zone is where growth and change happen. Making the world a better place for ourselves and those around us depends on us. You have a voice—even if only one person hears it. You have a voice…

What will you do with it?

End-of-Chapter Reflection

Chapter 14
Walking With God: Keys to Success

1. Name three keys to consistently and successfully walking with God.

_____

_____

_____

_____

_____

2. What are your biggest takeaways from Chapter 14?

_____

_____

_____

_____

_____

_____

_____

3. How will you incorporate what you learned from Chapter 14 into your life today (and moving forward)?

_____

_____

_____

_____

_____

_____

_____

4. Name something new that you discovered about yourself (if applicable).

_____

_____

_____

_____

_____

_____

_____

5. Name something new or interesting that you learned about God, life, and/or people (if applicable).

_____

_____

_____

_____

_____

_____

6. Journal any other notes, takeaways, or reminders that you'd like to capture from Chapter 14.

_____

_____

_____

_____

_____

_____

_____

_____

"'No eye has seen, no ear has heard, and no mind has imagined what God has prepared for those who love him.'"
1 Corinthians 2:9 NLT

Acknowledgements

My Heavenly Father

First and foremost, I have to thank my Lord and Savior Jesus Christ, giving all glory and honor to God. If it weren't for You, I wouldn't be the woman I am today, and this book never would've been written. I had no idea who I truly was or what my purpose was until I gave my life to You and gave You control of the wheel. Thank you for revealing Yourself to me through Your Word, for loving me, and for giving me direction, wisdom, discernment, and the opportunity and desire to dedicate my life to You. Thank You for every promise You've kept. I can see how every moment of my life was orchestrated by You, and I'm happy that all of the pieces led me to a realization of what life is really about. I could go on and on giving thanks and praise for all You've done for me. Thank You for everything You've done for me, Heavenly Father, big and small. I thank You for the good times and the bad, because it all had an effect that ultimately led me to You. You are my everything, and it's my pleasure and my heart's joy to give You all of me and to spend my life serving You and doing that which pleases You, not that which pleases man. Nothing compares to the peace and joy You have given me, as promised, for delighting myself in the Lord. I thank You, I love You always and forever. In the mighty Name of Jesus Christ, Amen.

My Kids

To my three amazing children Sean, Alanna, and Laila. I thank God for you. God gave me such a special gift when He gave me you. I am so happy to be your mommy, and I love you more than words can say. God used you to spark inspiration in me to write this book. You were the reason I started writing. I wanted you to know these things about God and life, and that desire grew into something that I desired to share with the world. Thank you for loving me and making life so easy for me as a mom. Thank you for listening to God when He says honor your parents, and thank you for always trying and doing your best. Thank you for helping me around the house and for listening to me when I give long speeches. Thank you for supporting me and for all of the sweet hugs and kisses you give me. I love you with all of my heart, and I hope you always remember to look to God, not the world, to guide you. Let God be the influencing factor in everything you do. Thank you again for being so super awesome. I love you always and forever.

My Mom

To my amazing mother Fran. Thank you for being the best mother a daughter could ask for. Thank you for teaching me, by example, to always strive for better. Thank you for teaching me to love myself and to never allow anyone to mistreat me. Thank you

for raising me to be strong and independent. Thank you for showing me what unconditional love and forgiveness looks like. Thank
you for always supporting, encouraging, and being there for me.
You always go above and beyond when it comes to people and the
ones you love, and I thank you for all you've done and for all you
do. Words can't express my love and gratitude for you. Most of
all, thank you for making sure I knew who God was. Thank you
for making sure I knew the importance of knowing God personally. I thank God for you. I love and appreciate you more than
words can say. Thank you, Mom.

My Sister

To my amazing sister Terraca. I love you so much, Sister. You
have such a big and beautiful heart. You are a ball of life—always
ready to live, laugh, and have a good time! You showed me what
generosity looks like. You are always ready and willing to give,
help, and support those you love, strangers included. I'm so
blessed to have a sister that is so loving, kind, strong, and smart.
Thank you for being you. I can barely find the words to express
how much I love and adore you, and I'm so grateful to have a sister
like you. I love you always.

Gerald Simmons

You lost your life to Covid-19 in 2021. This was something that
none of us expected. You have played such a major role in my life.
I called you "Dad" because that's what you were. You were like a
father to me from day one. You always loved and encouraged me.
You planted seeds in me that flourished and manifested in ways I

never knew until I got older and saw those seeds sprout. I thank God for sending you into my life. I never thought about taking honors classes until you suggested it. You saw things in me that I didn't see in myself or even think about. My first thought and words were, "Eww, why would I want to take harder classes?" Haha! But, because you opened my eyes to something greater, I graduated with honors and had an opportunity to see what I was actually capable of. That is just a fraction of the impact you've had in my life. You never failed to shower me with love and encouragement. You weren't just great to me, you were just as great to so many others. You always saw the best in others—things we didn't see in ourselves—and you never failed to make sure that anyone you encountered knew they were loved and had greatness in them. I thank you for everything. Thank you for being an example in my life of what unconditional, agape love and kindness looks like. Thank you for all of the love you gave to me and so many others. I hope you are resting in peace and enjoying the view up there. You will be forever loved and missed. Thank you, Dad. I love you.

My Aunt

To my amazing Aunt Cora. Thank you for being such a loving and supportive auntie. We have had so many laughs and good times! Thank you for giving me a Bible many years ago; the Bible that I talk so much about. The Living Bible (TLB). I can't even imagine what my life would be like if you had not given that Bible to me. Because it is so easy to understand, it has completely transformed my life. Thank you for always being there when I needed you and for all of the love and support you give! I love you to pieces! Thank you.

My Loving Family and Friends

Last, but most definitely not least! To my remaining close family and to my best of friends. Thank you for decades of genuineness, friendship, and love. It doesn't matter whether we talk every day or once in a while, we always pick up right where we left off without skipping a beat! Thank you for being a part of my life and for being so amazing! I'm so grateful to have you in my life. Words don't suffice. My life would not be the same nor as sweet without you! Each and every one of you is a blessing from God, and you have a very special place in my heart. May God bless, protect, and keep you, forever and ever. I thank God for you, and I love you always!

Additional Resources

The following FREE resources are a great addition as you continue along on your personal development journey. Take advantage!

You can download any of the free resources below at: www.LatinaNicholeSmith.com/free

The Bible, Where to Begin - My step-by-step guide.

Figuring out where to begin reading the Bible can be an overwhelming task, because we want to be sure we're going the best route for our spiritual growth. Although this varies from person to person, I'm sharing with you a free beginning-to-end, step-by-step guide that I followed when I began reading the Bible. I'm happy to help you along your journey as you get to know God and experience new life in Him. Visit www.LatinaNicholeSmith.com/free for your free guide.

Recommended Books - Books that changed my life!

We learned a lot in this book, and we discussed several areas we need to develop in order to elevate and escape a typical life of dysfunction. When it comes to these important characteristics—

positive thinking, good habits, mindset, and more—I have provided a list of books that you can read or listen to. They will help you strengthen and master these qualities along your personal development journey. Download a free list of my favorite books and why I recommend them at: www.LatinaNicholeSmith.com/free

End-Of-Chapter Reflection - Free fillable and printable PDF version!

You may download a free printable and fillable PDF version of the "End-of-Chapter Reflection" exercises at:

www.LatinaNicholeSmith.com/free

Gospel Playlist - My Favorites

On the next page you will find a list of my favorite gospel songs. A free printable PDF version is also available at:

www.LatinaNicholeSmith.com/free

Gospel Playlist
My Favorites

What we listen to and expose ourselves to plays a big part in our spiritual health and well being. Below is a list of my favorite Gospel songs. These powerful songs always give me encouragement, they make me feel closer to God, and they give me a sense of joy and peace within my soul. You can also find this list on my website as a downloadable PDF at:

www.LatinaNicholeSmith.com/free

I still love old school Gospel and I listen to it regularly. I hope you enjoy this list. I hope it warms your spirit and brings a sense of healing, peace, love, and calm to your soul, to your life, and to the space you occupy. Skip any song you don't like and meditate on the ones you love!

One of My All Time Favorites
"His Eye is on the Sparrow" by Mississippi Children's Choir

Healing
"Broken But I'm Healed" by Byron Cage
"Father Can You Hear Me" by Tiffany Evans, Cheryl Pepsii Riley, Terrell Carter

"Deliver Me (This Is My Exodus)" by The Tri-City Singers feat.
Le'Andria Johnson
"I Told the Storm" by Greg O'quin 'n' Joyful Noyze

Thankful
"Thank You" by Walter Hawkins
"I'm Blessed" by Charlie Wilson (feat. T.I.)
"We're Blessed" by Fred Hammond
"Grateful" by Hezekiah Walker & The Love Fellowship Choir

Encouraging/Uplifting
"God's Got a Blessing (With My Name on it)" by Norman
Hutchins
"Let Go (Radio Edit)" by DeWayne Woods
"Trouble Don't Last Always" by Rev Timothy Wright
"Be Encouraged" by William Becton
"Same Grace" by William Murphy
"Now Behold the Lamb" by Kirk Franklin
"That's What I Believe" by Donnie McClurkin
"More Than I Can Bear" by God's Property
"Safe In His Arms" by Milton Brunson
"Can't Give Up Now" by Mary Mary
"No Weapon" by Fred Hammond & Radical For Christ
"The Battle is the Lord's" by Yolanda Adams
"I'm Gonna Be Ready" by Yolanda Adams
"My Life is in Your Hands" by God's Property
"Blessing in the Storm" by Kirk Franklin

Set Free/God Kept Me/Saved Me
"That's When You Blessed Me" by The L.A. Mass Choir

"I Almost Let Go" by Kurt Carr & The Kurt Carr Singers

Praise
"I Love the Lord" by Whitney Houston
"Everlasting God" by William Murphy feat. Bishop James Morton
"You Are the Living Word (Live)" by Fred Hammond & Radical For Christ
"Silver and Gold" by Kirk Franklin

Praise/Encouraging/Protection/Upbeat
"Let The Praise Begin (Live)" by Fred Hammond & Radical For Christ
"Jesus Be A Fence" by Fred Hammond & Radical For Christ
"Jesus Can Work It Out" by Cosmopolitan Church of Prayer Choir

Don't ever allow your mind to dwell on negative thoughts. Always direct your thoughts towards positivity, and train your mind to always think about things that lift you up, not things that bring you down.

"Finally, brethren, whatever things are true, noble, just, pure, lovely, and are of good report, if there is any virtue and if there is anything praiseworthy—meditate on these things."
Philippians 4:8 NKJV

Why I Wrote This Book
A Mother's Love

After spending a few decades in this life, I noticed a great deal of dysfunction, chaos, and confusion in the world. There were things I wanted my children to know about the world and life, but they were still very young. *What if something happens to me and they find themselves lost in this crazy world?* I thought. *What if I'm not here to talk to them or teach them important things about life when they need it the most?* These thoughts were very unsettling for me, and for some reason, they lingered.

Problem detected, solution elected!

That's how my brain works. So, I started writing down everything I wanted my children to know about life and how to handle, or avoid, many of the issues we encounter.

This book started out as a letter to them; thereby, if anything ever happened to me, God forbid, I would be able to speak to them and teach them as if I were still around. They would still be able to turn to me—my words—and hear from me, no matter what. They wouldn't have to feel lost or confused about life. The thought of this gave my heart great comfort, joy, and peace.

While writing, the keys I wanted my kids to know became something I wanted every child to know—and the keys I wanted every child to know became something I wanted everyone to know.

And so, out of love and from the heart, this book was born. All of which was orchestrated by God.

The Lord is always finding different ways to reach us. I don't believe you stumbled upon this book by accident. You are a very special person, and you are loved by your Creator and Heavenly Father. I pray that God showers His presence, His blessings, and His favor upon you and your life.

To God be the glory and honor, forever and ever.
Amen.

To My Children
Sean, Alanna, and Laila

Hi kids, my loves, Sean, Alanna, and Laila. I love you so much. You guys always tell me I talk too much. Well, it turns out it's a gift! I love teaching you things. The more you know, the more prepared you are for any situation in life.

I hope the way I chose to live and the messages I left behind will lead you to a peaceful, happy, and prosperous life. I hope they will teach you the power of *choice,* and I hope your lives will be full of good choices.

The most important *choice* of all is choosing to look to God and His Word to lead you in every decision you make. Choosing righteousness over anything else and living God's way will always protect you and lead you in the direction of peace, love, happiness, favor, and prosperity.

The ability to speak to you forever, through this book, brings my heart great joy. Life can be hard, but it doesn't always have to be. When you apply the type of knowledge and wisdom that I aim to bestow upon you, your life will be so much easier, enjoyable, fulfilling, and the list goes on. Even during hard times, you will be protected and remain filled with peace and joy when you know the things I have written in this book and have always taught you.

I love you more than words could ever say. Please bring my heart joy by choosing to trust in God always, no matter what happens. Choose to be a good person, no matter what other people do. This will ensure you receive the greatest reward that life has to offer from our Creator, Lord, and Savior above! I love you. Forever and always. Always and forever, Mommy.

"Trust in the LORD with all your heart and lean not unto your own understanding. In all your ways acknowledge Him and He will direct your paths."
Proverbs 3:5-6

About the Author

LATINA NICHOLE SMITH is an author, mentor, and mother of three who currently resides in Central Florida. She enjoys teaching others how to apply God's Word and Wisdom to life so they can develop a *personal* relationship with the Lord and escape the typical life of emptiness, confusion, dysfunction, and defeat. She understands how excruciating it is to go through life feeling lost, lonely, and confused—and she knows exactly how to turn it around. For that reason, she found joy and purpose in utilizing her God-given gift of wisdom to help others find their way out of the dark.

To those who know her best, Latina is a devoted mother who is calm-spirited and wise beyond her years. She loves writing, spreading the Good News, traveling the world, nice weather, and powdery white sand beaches with vibrant palm trees and clear blue water. Ahhhh. Just hearing those last words makes you feel warm, fuzzy, and relaxed.

Website and Social Media

If you enjoyed reading Biblical Keys to Life, stay connected with the author and be the first to receive updates on new releases, valuable new resources, events, and upcoming book releases by visiting www.LatinaNicholeSmith.com. Connect with and follow the author regularly on social media at:

Blog: www.LatinaNicholeSmith.com
Facebook: www.Facebook.com/LatinaNicholeSmith
YouTube: @LatinaNicholeSmith
Instagram: @LatinaNicholeSmith
Twitter: @LatinaNichole

For information on bulk order discounts, speaking events, or other inquiries, email: info@LuvheirPublishing.com

Index